*A funny thing happened
on the way to the Clubhouse*

A Funny Thing
happened

edited by Robert Anderson
cartoons by Doug Smith

on the way to the Clubhouse

ARTHUR BARKER LIMITED
5 Winsley Street London W1

ISBN 0 213 99388 0

Printed Web Offset in Great Britain by
R Kingshott & Co Ltd, Aldershot, Hants

Contents

1   Nicked a New Pair of Socks!   7
    Peter Dobereiner

2   Practice Loses the Lot   15
    Patrick Campbell

3   In the Drink   26
    Henry Longhurst

4   Golf is a Funny Game   31
    Ronald Heager

5   Par and the Puritans   50
    George Houghton

6   Liberty, Sorority, Equality!   61
    Henry Longhurst

7   The Golf Course   66
    Michael Green

8   The Perils of Broadcasting   74
    Tom Scott

9   The Common Touch   85
    Steve Roberts

10 By the Right, Dress!   94
    Robert Anderson

11 Either You Laugh or You Don't   100
    Patrick Smartt

12 How Lucky We Are   110
    Geoffrey Cousins

13 What is Golf?   119
    Webster Evans

1 Nicked a New Pair of Socks!

Peter Dobereiner

Caddies, they keep telling us, are a dying race and to judge strictly by appearances few people would care to dispute that diagnosis. Watching them assembled outside the pro's shop on a tournament morning I sometimes get the feeling that time has slipped a cog and like a new Bridie Murphy I have been transplanted back into history.

For this, surely, must be something pretty closely resembling the scene when the straggling remnants of Napoleon's army finally made it back from Moscow. Their raggle-taggle clothes, cast-offs and mostly ill fitting, help the impression of refugee disorder. And the few who are smartly turned out – the aristocrats of the calling whose appearance would not disgrace the locker room of an American professional event – must be the officers who have travelled by coach.

But it is the physical condition of the rank and file which most strongly suggests combat and deprivation. Fresh wounds, old bruises turning parchment coloured at the edges, and bleary eyes picked out in vivid shades of crimson heighten the fantasy.

These are the men, however, who day after day hump bags of clubs too heavy for most mortals to transport further than from car boot to trolley for distances up to ten miles. Although they look to be in the extremes of mortal disintegration they nevertheless perform feats of endurance which would shame the general run of spade-leaning navvies.

How do they do it? Well, I can now reveal that they have a rigorous training scheme which has been evolved over the centuries and which makes the normal commando course look like a nursery tea party. It is, of course, a closely guarded secret and I only know about it because I have been able to piece together odd little facts, a hint dropped here and there. And *no other explanation fits the known facts*.

The course is divided into two main sections: Physical Training and Mental Agility. Let us first examine the hitherto undisclosed details of their methods of toughening the physique. Diet is the key; they live exclusively on water, sugar for energy, nourishing malt, and a herb of the genus Humulus sometimes known as hops. (I have not yet cracked the secret of how these ingredients are mixed but I believe the process involves a technique of infusion and fermentation.)

This simple fare breeds men of astonishing longevity and induces a trancelike state which gives them the strength and courage to perform miraculous feats beyond the normal human limits. It is not possible for the caddies

If he'd only *pretend* it was difficult

to keep their toughening-up exercises entirely free from public scrutiny so they go to elaborate lengths to pretend they are doing something else. Perhaps the best way I can explain their method is to give an actual example from a recent Open championship.

By an administrative oversight two visiting players from overseas arrived to find that each had been allotted two caddies. At that late hour there was no time to make fresh arrangements and so two poor caddies were left without bags to carry. Such is the freemasonry among these fellows that after the championship, meeting in convivial conclave, the general body of caddies decided that the two who had worked (and been generously rewarded by their American bosses) should share their spoils with the two who, through no fault of their own, had been left unemployed for the week.

A share-out was duly made and the beneficiaries were humbly grateful. At this point the touching tale becomes even more touching. The two caddies who had worked hurried to the club, found their masters and told them how they had opened their hearts and shared their emoluments among the two unfortunates. The Americans were impressed at this example of brotherhood. 'But,' said one, 'it was not necessary in this instance. We had already paid the other two in full, they have been amply recompensed for it was not their fault that they were unable to work.' Oh the generosity of the human spirit! One cannot help but be moved.

'Oh, *really*?' said the two caddies, and hurried back to the licensed premises where the fraternity was gathered. Can you guess what next transpired? They had a training session in which every bag carrier participated, performing their superhuman feats of strength with such gusto that by next morning not a single piece of the furnishings nor any window remained intact. And two of the participants (by coincidence they were the same two who had been paid twice for not working) had to undergo a period of convalescence.

Another old caddie, now alas sitting contentedly on the bench outside the hut of the Great Caddiemaster in the Sky, became so deeply immersed in trance that his inert body presented something of a problem to his fellows at the end of an evening's training session. They picked him up, hoisted his rigid frame to their shoulders and bore him to the golf course where preparations were afoot for the coming tournament. They found a marquee, folded and dumped on the grass ready for erection the next morning. Prising apart the heavy folds of canvas they inserted their friend into the recesses of the tent, much as one slips a card into an envelope. Came the dawn and with it the contractor's men who, unfolding the tent, discovered the body and remarked laconically: 'Hello, we must have folded him up in there by accident when we took down the tent at the Agfa last week.'

By means of such toughening up processes caddies are able to survive any eventuality they are liable to meet on the course, such as a recent occurrence in America when an exasperated golfer hurled his bag of clubs over a bridge into a river and promptly despatched his caddie in like manner after them.

But if their bodies are hard so too are their minds and this is achieved through learning by heart a vast number of conversational responses, mostly of Scottish origin, to cover any contingency. Sir Walter Simpson laid it down as an essential of the caddie's duties that he manages to 'conceal his just contempt for your game'. There spoke an amateur. It is a matter of professional pride to the caddie that he *reveals* his utter contempt for your game no matter how unjustified it may be. Break the course record with a 64 and a real caddie will congratulate you on your good fortune. 'Of course, with your game you need all the luck that's going.'

Two new verbal gambits have been introduced recently to the caddie repertory. An American visiting St Andrews told his venerable carrier: 'I've heard about you guys. My money buys transport and silence. That's all. I don't want the lines and I don't want advice on clubbing.'

They set off and the visitor was all over the place, wildly off line with every shot. After six holes he capitulated. 'OK, OK, OK,' he said, 'what's the way to play this next hole.'

'First of all,' said the caddie evenly, 'is it the Old, or the New, or the Jubilee or the Eden we're supposed to be playing?'

And this year's Captain of the PGA, Hugh Lewis, relates how he plucked a few strands of grass and threw them in the air to gauge the wind and asked his caddie, 'What club do you think?'. His man, who happened to be standing downwind and had received a couple of blades of grass in his hair, bent down, tore a clod from

– And I wish to pay tribute to the sporting way in which my opponent took his crushing defeat

the fairway, threw it directly into Lewis's face and answered quietly: 'I don't know.'

These are just a few of the numerous incidents which prove that, far from dying out, the caddies of today are as strong and resilient as ever. Their techniques are improving all the time as new survival tricks are discovered. Earlier this year one old caddie was limping horribly through his morning round and my interest was quickly aroused when I saw him marching as proudly as a Guardsman after lunch. That evening I overheard him tell one of his fellows, 'I've cured those feet – nicked a new pair of socks.'

By such scientific discoveries is the storehouse of survival wisdom enriched. There is, as I see it, no danger at all of the British caddie dying out. For my own part I propose now to embark on a new investigation; I have a feeling that there is a gigantic conspiracy involving the ruling bodies of every other sport. Alarmed at the drift from cricket, hockey and football to golf they are secretly subsidizing the caddies so that they can more effectively pursue their activities as *agents provocateurs*.

2 Practice Loses the Lot

Patrick Campbell

In the ordinary golf club where, perhaps, about a hundred members might play regularly, three of them are figures of fun.

They are the ones – the proportion is usually about 3 per cent – who use the practice ground for the purpose of improving their game.

The other 97 wouldn't dream of going near it. Like 97 per cent of all golfers everywhere they believe that next time out, for reasons to be analysed later in the bar, they will play the game of their lives. It will just come, out of the blue, and stay with them for ever. They feel that there is no point in practising, seeing that this miraculous improvement is guaranteed by Fate.

There may be something to be said for them, in view of the fact that the 3 per cent who do practise, practise a game which they are exceedingly unlikely to play on the course.

I recall a time – it was Hogan's *Power Golf* that did

it to me again – when I resolved to rebuild my game from the ground up with a rigorous course of practice in the garden. A hundred shots before breakfast, lunch, tea and dinner – that sort of thing.

I bought a practice net, rigged between two poles supported by guy ropes, and set it up in such a way that a loose one would fly harmlessly into a neighbouring field. I then cut out from *Power Golf* the series of photographs depicting Hogan at work with his driver and pasted them, in sequence, on a sheet of cardboard. This meant buying two copies of *Power Golf*, to get the photographs on the back of the preceding page, but it was plain the expense was going to be worth it.

I started to practise, then, with the series of photographs tacked to a neighbouring tree.

Power golf took over immediately. The first shot with the driver was so powerful that it went clean through the netting and disappeared into the field, leaving a large hole behind it. The netting, as far as I could make out, must have been intended for the reception of tiny iron shots played by very young girls, so I dug some disused under-felt out of the beams of the garage and draped that over the netting, as an additional fortification. The weight pulled the guy ropes out of the ground and the whole thing fell down. The miserable little pegs provided by the manufacturers were clearly inadequate. I substituted some old iron bars, hammered them a couple of feet down into the lawn and set up the whole fortified apparatus all over again. It now looked sufficiently robust to defy a tank.

You'll notice his partners rarely miss a putt

The next shot with the driver missed it altogether. In the Hogan style I had my chin well cocked and the head right down at the moment of impact, so that I never saw where it went. After waiting for what felt like an hour for the crash of glass or a cry of pain I guessed that the ball had found some harmless destination. Rather than have the same period of anxiety again I moved much closer to the net for the next one and was rewarded by a solid thunk as the ball hit the under-felt. The first one had probably passed right over the top of it.

A hundred shots later I found that the lawn had taken a lot of punishment, particularly from the push with the inside of the right foot at the moment of impact, but there was no doubt at all that extra power was here. Holes were beginning to appear in the under-felt, even after I'd hung a bedspread over it to take the initial shock.

It was, as may be imagined, with high expectation that I took this new swing on to the golf course the following Saturday morning, going so far as to tell my caddy that I was ' doing it the Hogan way now '.

Big, wide arc going back, dragging the hands down to initiate the down swing, hips going round to face the hole and a pistol-like crack as the club-face met the ball. Missing the familiar thunk as it hit the under-felt, I looked up to see where the drive had gone and could find no trace of it in the surrounding scenery.

I looked at my caddy, in search of a clue, and saw his mouth open. He was staring, in astonishment, in the direction of cover point. Following his eyeline, at about

45° to the intended line of flight, I saw the ball passing quail-high, having carried more than 200 yards, over a distant hedge and out of bounds.

This, with the rigid Hogan left arm, turned out to have been the shot I'd been practising with such devotion all week, deprived by the nearness of the netting, however, from seeing its ultimate development. It was another week before I was able to to bend one back on to the course again.

Practice with a net, therefore, should be attempted only by players so expert that they can tell, purely by feel, where the shot has gone, and if there are any of those around I wouldn't mind meeting them.

The practice ground is a wiser investment for the ordinary player. At least here he can see the result, but he's going to need a caddy to pick them up.

Without a caddy practice is likely to be brought to a premature end through lack of ammunition, as we shall see in:

CASE HISTORY

Jack is a large and powerfully built young man who has been playing golf for two years, and sees it as the only human activity of any worth.

He is so keen, indeed, that he refuses to join in a jolly Sunday morning fourball, in favour of what he calls 'a work-out' on the practice ground.

He's been reading too many American golf books.

What Americans mean by 'a work-out' is a flexing

of their superbly trained muscles in the reproduction of the same shot over and over again.

What Jack means by 'a work-out', though he doesn't know it, is a series of experiments, using half a dozen different styles, in an attempt to hit six successive shots comparatively straight.

It's a blustery morning, with the wind blowing across the practice ground and the morning sun still rather low at the eastern end.

Jack starts off with the sun behind him, tipping about a dozen balls out of the bag and taking a 4-iron.

He's never quite sure how far a 4-iron is going to go, so he plays a nice easy one in the general direction of the other end of the practice ground. The result, inconceivably, is a socket. The ball disappears almost at right angles into the undergrowth bordering the practice ground about thirty yards away.

Jack looks round cautiously to see if he has been observed. Several of his fellow members – the lazy incompetents who can never be bothered to practise though God knows they need it – have jeered at his enthusiasm before now.

Four of them, naturally enough, have been privileged to see Jack's opening shot from half-way down the first fairway. They call out encouraging advice. 'No need to practise that one, Jack, you've got it made.' And so on. They stand there, with four caddies, making an audience of eight, to watch his next one.

Determined to avoid another socket, and jokes which will take a week to die, Jack keeps his head right down

Yes, I estimate she's a 36! Oh! – You mean her handicap

on this one and hits the ball a good, firm blow with his right hand. It feels all right, but it's disappeared by the time he looks up to follow its flight. The chorus of derision from the audience gives him no clue to its direction. Jack makes a mental note to look for it in the short rough on the left.

Some minutes later, at the other end of the practice ground, Jack wishes he'd counted his total of balls more carefully. He's nearly sure he'd started with about twelve, but now there seem to be only eight left. He remembers the one he socketed into the bushes. That makes nine. Jack decides the others will probably turn up, and hits three shots back into the sun. He sees nothing of any of them, but they didn't feel too bad, so he knocks up the other five.

At the other end of the practice ground there is no sign of any golf balls at all. All eight practice shots have vanished without a trace and the practice ground is nearly a hundred yards wide.

After a long search Jack finds the first one – the one he knocked into the bushes – and three more at widely spaced intervals in the rough on either side.

If he has any sense, having lost eight balls in ten minutes, he will now withdraw to the putting green in front of the clubhouse where, even if he doesn't do his putting any good, another half-hour's practice will leave him with the same amount of ammunition as he started with.

This is the only benefit that can come to someone who practises by himself.

Scientific practice – which will probably revolutionize

one's whole game – can be enjoyed only with the help of a caddy to pick up the spray of stuff which tends to emerge.

The caddy, however, must be prepared to cover considerable distances at a trot and should therefore be under fifteen years of age.

Older caddies actually hinder practice.

On one occasion, sharpening up for the Halford Hewitt at Deal, I got one who must have been approaching seventy, as a result of negotiations with the caddy master, which have taken the same form for years.

'I've had the blanket on him all night. He's full of bran mash and rarin' to go. Give us your harness and we'll strap it on.'

On this occasion, after we'd strapped the harness on to the seventy-year-old horse, I told him we'd go down to the practice ground 'for a bit of a loosen up', as we weren't off for another hour.

The old man looked at me with loathing, an attention he'd already paid to my bag of clubs. He humped them on to his shoulder, raised his red-rimmed eyes to the sky and stumped off to the practice ground, followed at a discreet distance by myself.

When we arrived it was to find a number of the stars of the tournament, including several Blues, already rifling shots far into the distance. I chose an empty space well away from them.

My caddy lowered the bag to the ground and started, with a patent machine, to roll himself a very thin and shaggy cigarette.

'Perhaps,' I said, 'you'd like to get out there and pick up a few shots –?'

He completed his manufacture of the cigarette, lit it, put his hands in the pockets of his voluminous overcoat and set off.

About a hundred yards away he turned and stood looking at me mournfully, the hands still in his overcoat pockets.

I made various signs indicating that I wanted him to go farther away. After a long time he shrugged hopelessly, turned on his fallen arches and retreated about another fifty yards.

I took out the driver and hit a beauty, well over his head. He made no movement of any kind. It was clear he hadn't seen it at all.

I did a lot more waving, trying to drive him still farther back. After nearly a minute he seemed to get my meaning and plodded off again, nearly out of sight against the ditch bordering the far field.

The second shot was a lot less effective than the first – a quick hook which nearly decapitated one of the Blues' caddies and disappeared into the field on the left.

My eagle-eyed horse didn't see that one either.

Of the next dozen shots five of them finished in the field, two were topped and the remainder were pushed miles out to the right. The five in the field were wisely ignored by my helper who was, however, good enough to pick up the others. It took him a long time as they weren't exactly together. In mid-trek across the practice ground he paused at one moment to confer with his colleague, who scarcely had to move at all to pick up his master's contribution. I judged he was telling him that you get all sorts in the Halford Hewitt.

When he returned to me, with what remained of our supplies, he put them straight back in the bag, picked it up and stumped off to the first tee. Though we still had another half-hour to go it was clear that our loosening-up process was over.

Practice, then, to be perfect needs an overcast day, a fleet-footed young retriever and, I should say, the attendance of at least one assistant professional to keep the player up to scratch – or as close to it as he is ever likely to get.

I've never been really devoted to it myself, not since the morning Henry Longhurst caught me at it at Lytham St Annes.

He watched me play half a dozen not absolutely immaculate mid-irons. Then he spoke.

'It will take you,' he said, 'at least seventy-nine shots to get round. If I were you I wouldn't waste any of them here. You're liable to run out of steam.'

From *How To Become A Scratch Golfer* (Bland)

3 In the Drink
Henry Longhurst

Speaking at a dinner, Mr P. B. Lucas, DSO, DFC, recalled that he had previously been invited to speak at the dinner of the same society's swimming club and proceeded to analyse the surprisingly close association between golf – if not golfers – and water. It proved to be a fruitful theme, with which in a golfing career that began at the age of five he could claim a fairly varied connection.

He mentioned Pine Valley, which he visited with the 1936 Walker Cup team, though without in fact playing in the match. This is a great 'water' course, with one short hole a complete island except for a single narrow footpath and another with a vast carry over a lake.

Here he was so often in woods or water that an American paper entitled him the 'Southpaw sprayer'. I should add perhaps in fairness that another speaker at the dinner referred to him, and I think rightly, as 'the only left-hander who ever looked like a golfer'.[1]

[1] This, I need hardly say, was before New Zealander Bob Charles won the 1963 Open Championship.

In a pro-amateur tournament in Florida, he went on, his professional partner sliced into a creek at the eighteenth and found his ball in a flat-bottomed boat, which he solemnly punted to a position level with the green, chipped out of, and holed the putt for a four.

Perhaps his most engaging reminiscence was of the occasion when he was 'knocked off' by a cannon shell at 30,000 feet while returning from escorting an American raid on Lille. As he was contemplating jumping out of his Spitfire, losing stroke and distance, the white cliffs of Ramsgate hove in view, reminding him that he knew every inch of the course at Prince's, Sandwich – indeed he was born in the clubhouse – and could perhaps put the machine down on the first fairway.

He overshot this, and then the old sixth, and then the ninth – farthest point of the course – and eventually came to rest in a ditch in the marsh – out of bounds yet again!

Water engenders more violent emotions in the golfer's heart than any other hazard. The futility of hitting it into the pond, followed by the slow humiliation of having to fish it out with a wire contraption on the end of a pole, or worse still being able to see it but not reach it, certain in the knowledge that some enterprising small boy will have gone in and got it by the morning, gives one what the Americans call the 'slow burn' to a degree unmatched by the fiercest heather or gorse.

Many occasions come to mind. I did not see the Oxford player who flung his clubs into the lake at Stoke Poges, but I did see a Cambridge undergraduate knee-deep in the stream beside the fifth at Mildenhall, trying to retrieve his putter in order to continue playing in the Trials – and, furthermore, I once met a fellow who claimed to be the original of the story of the man who, after an unsuccessful foray in Scotland, flung his clubs into the Firth of Forth one by one from the carriage window, followed by the bag.

The Swilcan Burn at St Andrews has been the scene, of course, of innumerable tragi-comedies of golf, none better than that of the man who, playing it as the nineteenth, fluffed into it three times. He threw his clubs in, so it is said; then he threw his caddie in; then jumped in himself. The only man really to get the better of the Burn, as I like to think, was a celebrated Australian professional. He dismissed it with the comment that he had ' got in the drink at the first '.

One water hazard which took its place in history almost before it was built is the artificial kidney-shaped pond, already stocked with fish, into which poor Harry Weetman hit his second shot at the last hole during the Ryder Cup match at Eldorado. This was one of seven or eight similar hazards guarding the four greens that border on the clubhouse and one of the reasons for installing them, instead of sand, was to prevent players from 'skimming' shots by mistake into the assembled company on the terrace.

Many of the professionals, especially the Americans who are so adept at splashing out of sand bunkers, gnashed their teeth at the very sight of them and declared them to be unfair, but to me they were the greatest of

Watch Him! – He's an expert at the nose-nudge

fun and I should like to see golf enlivened by more of them. But then I wasn't playing in the match.

From *Always On Sunday* (Cassell)

4 Golf is a Funny Game

Ronald Heager

'Golf is a funny game, caddie.'

'Aye, sir, but it's no' meant to be.'

The old time Scot was showing the true regard of his race for the royal and ancient pastime. But truth is the game has been contradicting him ever since it began. Golf *is* funny. It just cannot help itself.

Take Arnold Palmer, most regal golfer of his age. The first time I met him was on his visit to Portmarnock for the 1960 Canada Cup. He was US Masters and Open Champion, on the crest of a wave. It was his first taste of British conditions. The golf writers swarmed round him at the end of his first practice round. Deftly, good-humouredly, Arnie answered all the questions.

Inevitably he was asked: 'What about the small ball, how do you get on with it?' Palmer added a regiment of friends to his 'Army' with the reply:

'I like the small ball. It makes the hole look bigger.'

I have found Arnie's off-the-cuff quips and repartee rolling forth ever since. Even in his blackest moments.

After the Open Championship triumphs of Royal Birkdale and Troon, Palmer had to strike his colours at Royal Lytham in 1963. He never got his game going and finished joint twenty-sixth.

On the final day the outgoing champion endured the indignity of an early starting time at the back of the field while Bob Charles, Phil Rodgers, Jack Nicklaus and Peter Thomson fought it out for the title. I was among a band of loyalists on hand to greet Palmer as he finished his fourth round in 76.

The path from the eighteenth green ran between the ivy-clad, red-brick clubhouse and a temporary television tower. Arnie strode in with his card, tight-lipped and grim. But as he drew abreast of the tower he saw a few familiar faces and with an upward glance at the tubular scaffolding he remarked laconically:

'Is this where you hang yourself?'

The Palmer stories are legion. My favourite is related by former Walker Cup player Guy Wolstenholme.

Guy, in his second year as a professional, began a tour of the American winter circuit in January 1962. It lasted three weeks, tragically cut short by an accident in which Guy broke his left arm.

It happened at Cypress Point, one of the three famous Pacific Coast courses on which the annual Bing Crosby tournament is played. Guy, in his last practice round, jumped on to what appeared to be the stump of a tree. It turned out to be a loose log which gave way and sent Guy crashing to the ground.

The scene was the tee of the sixth hole, one of the

Get in there and try to pick out who signed these bar chits Chou en Lai and Mickey Mouse

toughest and most renowned par three's in golf. It is 222 yards, a full drive across the yawning blue waters of the Pacific to a peninsula green. If you miss the green, it's down the cliff into the foaming seas below.

After the accident a woebegone Wolstenholme, with arm strapped up, encountered Arnold Palmer. Arnie consoled Guy and said: 'I always knew it was one helluva hole, but I did not realize it was so tough it could break your arm!'

Palmer's great American rival, Jack Nicklaus, looks just as stern and serious as Arnold while taking a golf course apart. Yet Jack, too, has a sharp and spontaneous wit.

The second round of the 1964 Open Championship was a disaster for him. He was blown out of it with a round of 74, containing 40 putts, the most he had ever had in a tournament. Next morning he made his move in what proved to be the vain chase of Tony Lema with a scorching third round of 66.

Before Jack began the final round, an American journalist, Tom Reedy, encountered him in the Royal and Ancient clubhouse and said:

'Well, Jack, I see you've discovered the secret of the Old Course.'

Replied Nicklaus, with a grin: 'Yes. Fewer putts.'

Nicklaus visited England for the Piccadilly tournament at Southport in his first year as a professional in 1962. We were old acquaintances from the Walker Cup matches at Muirfield and Seattle. We talked of this and that and I said: 'Where was your last tournament, Jack?'

'At Burneyville, Oklahoma. Just a place with two houses,' he replied.

'Good course?' I asked.

'Just like you'd get at a place with two houses,' was Jack's all-embracing reply.

All the fun of the fairways is no monopoly of the Americans, even though the flamboyant Walter Hagen contributed more than his share in another era. It is not the monopoly of the moderns, either.

Like the best of golf and golfers, some of the loveliest stories come from Scotland. The hero of every other one of them is the legendary Andra' Kirkaldy, a rugged native of St Andrews with a salty turn of phrase. Frank Moran, doyen of golf writers and fifty years the *Scotman*'s correspondent, has a treasure house of Scots stories. I retell three of them.

The craggy, powerful Kirkaldy formed a colourful partnership with 'Wee Ben' Sayers, for more than forty years the golfing monarch of that other famous citadel of the game, North Berwick.

They played many important matches together around the turn of the century. One of them was at St Andrews at a time when the railway line bordering the right of the fifteenth and sixteenth holes was not out of bounds as it is now. Sayers cut his shot on to the lines, giving Kirkaldy a horrible lie among the sleepers and flints.

Andra' was far from pleased. He climbed the railings, saying: 'This is a time for sweerin'. Staund back, you wimmen.'

The diminutive Sayers came over to the railings as

35

Kirkaldy fumed over the lie, in time to hear Andra' say:
'Lend us that wee mashie of yours.'

'Na, na,' replied Ben. 'Brek yer ain bluidy club.'

Kirkaldy's challenge matches with Sayers took them
all over the country. Once Andra' was one of a quartet
seeking a restaurant in the West End of London. They
eventually settled for what the itinerant professionals
would have classified as a 'posh' place. The meal was
excellent. But the bill was a stunner. As the party left, an
obsequious and slightly anxious waiter helped Andra' on
with his coat and murmured:

'You won't forget the waiter, sir?'

'Naw,' Kirkaldy answered huffily. 'Ah'll never forget
ye. And what's more, ah'll never forgie ye!'

St Andrews is as inseparable from the fun of the game
as it is from golf itself. The Old Course has a short hole
which few would challenge as being the greatest par
three in the world, the 170-yard eleventh, with its Shell
and Cockle bunkers, the estuary of the Eden at the
back, and the fiendish slope of the green towards the
tee.

One of the pillars of golf as a pastime early in the
century was the Rt Hon A. J. Balfour, a leading politic-
ian who probably did as much for the game in Britain as
President Eisenhower was to do later in the United
States.

Mr Balfour was a regular visitor to North Berwick
and St Andrews. At the time he was Secretary of State
for Ireland, his golfing excursions demanded the attendance of a couple of armed detectives. It all helped to

publicize golf and make people think there must be something in the game. It also left the locals of St Andrews in no doubt about the importance of Mr Balfour.

One day Balfour was playing the Old Course and duly reached the short eleventh. His tee shot found the green but he was left with a long, long, difficult putt. He consulted his caddie about the line and was told:

'Hit it a yaird to the left.'

The ball finished a good yard to the right of the flag. Whereon the caddie snorted to a companion:

'And these are the b . . . . . s that are running the country.'

There is no end to the classic caddie comments. Among my favourites is that during the club consultation routine between hacker and caddie at a hole where the tee shot has to traverse a lake.

'What shall I take here?' queries the player, gravely.

'An old ball,' is the brutal reply.

Then there is the pun to end all puns from the Scots caddie wearied at too frequent replacing of divots:

'It's no' replacing the tur-r-f I am. It's retur-r-fing the bluidy place.'

The companion one to this is:

Player: 'I'll move heaven and earth to play this game properly.'

Caddie (a few holes later): 'Well, 'e's only got 'eaven ter move now.'

Bad-tempered golfers and bland caddies are a prolific source of golfing fun. Few match this gem:

'You must be the worst caddie in the world.'

'Gawd, no, sir. That would be too much of a co-incidence.'

It is said the Scots themselves invent tales like that in which the Scots golfer asked his boy caddie: 'Are you guid at finding balls?'

'Aye, sir.'

'Away then and find one and we'll start the game.'

Thirty years ago Henry Longhurst, who has a most perceptive ear and joyous pen for the lighter side of golf, collaborated with Robert Graves on an anthology of caddie stories, *Candid Caddies*.

The one I cherish most from their researches concerns the Colonel given to explosive language on the course. His efforts to curb the violent expression of his wrath reached the stage of giving his straitlaced, chapel-going caddie a sixpenny fine for every oath.

The old man was said to flinch with horror at his master's outbursts. But he made sure of collecting the sixpences.

At the end of one round the Colonel made his calculation and handed over 4s. 6d. for his cuss words.

The old man counted it and said: 'Beg pardon, Colonel, but ain't ye forgotten the b..... on the fourth green?'

The caddies are vanishing. But the fun goes on.

Mention of Henry Longhurst brings back memory of a gorgeous aside he made at the 1959 Ryder Cup match in America. The opulent background of the Eldorado Country Club – members, President Eisenhower, Bing

I'm *terribly* sorry! ⌐ Did that piercing blast on my trumpet disturb you?

Crosby, Bob Hope – gave the Americans the perfect setting for putting on the show they love at golf's international occasions.

Among the amenities was the band of an American Air Force unit. They confined their efforts, of course, to the morning flag-raising ceremony and the luncheon interval. During lunch one of the tunes they played was what the airmen no doubt knew as the theme music from that splendid war film, 'Bridge on the River Kwai'. The British party thought of it as the rousing, ribald 'Colonel Bogey' march.

As Longhurst and I walked past the band, Henry remarked tartly: 'I wonder if they know the words?'

The late Bernard Darwin, Longhurst's predecessor as a golfing laureate, contrived his mellifluous essays and reports with a gentle, chiding humour which mirrored his life-long affair with the game of golf.

Darwin was an accomplished player – Walker Cup, England, Cambridge University – but if things went wrong on the course he had a reputation for exploding into a raging fury. His imprecations had to be heard to be believed, say those who knew him.

Beset with bunker trouble one day, he was heard to invoke the Lord to damn and blast the bunker to everlasting hell-fire. And as a rider to his oaths he raged:

'... And don't send your Son down. This is a man's job.'

An event specially cherished by Darwin was the President's Putter, which he won in 1924. This hardy

annual winter frolic of the Oxford and Cambridge Golfing Society ranks second to none in the standard of its
gaiety, humour and wit.

The participants, men honoured and respected in the
highest walks of life, enjoy the nicknames of their youth.
Each year the entry will contain: 'The Emperor', 'The
Poet', 'The Monk', 'The Camel', 'The Italian', and
the like.

In a recent 'Putter' Donald Steel was playing another
past winner, Michael Anderson, a doctor from Liverpool,
in a third round tie so desperately fought that it went to
the sixth extra hole, the twenty-fourth.

As the large gallery surged onward from the twenty-
fourth tee the talk turned to the possibility of calling a
halt because of failing light. This brought up the question
of the longest match in the history of the event, that in
which Tony Duncan defeated John Beck at the twenty-
sixth hole in 1948. This duel was halted by darkness,
Duncan winning on the resumption in the morning and
going on to win the final.

I was reporting the Steel-Anderson match and was
able to check all the facts of the 1948 marathon with
John Beck himself, who was walking in the crowd beside
me. I shall always remember his concluding remark:
'We had to stop not so much because we could not see
the flags, but because we could not see each other.'

This was in the highest tradition of the event, which
January's rawest weather has only once prevented finishing on schedule.

Gerald Micklem, staunchest of Oxford and Cambridge

golf supporters, has done everything and met everybody who is anybody in the game. From his term as Walker Cup captain he reveals a delicious anecdote which displays how in some ways Britain and America live in two worlds of golf.

A prelude to the Walker Cup matches is always a joint conference of the teams to make clear the conditions and form of the match and any small differences existing between R & A and USGA rules.

In 1957 when the match was at Minikahda the teams duly assembled. Some of the Americans had to be carefully briefed about the foursomes, a form of golf rare in the United States.

As the explanation regarding playing alternate strokes drew to an end one of the newcomers to the American side put the ultimate question: 'Does it mean if my partner holes the putt, I drive off at the next tee?'

In the ghastly hush that followed this boner, the abashed player asked his captain, Charlie Coe: 'Do I still play in the foursomes tomorrow, captain?'

He did. His name – Arnold Blum.

In the 1955 Walker Cup match at St Andrews I recollect watching the morning singles beside the thirteenth green in the company of a group including the American captain, the charming 'Big Bill' Campbell, who as recently as 1964 won the American Amateur title at the age of forty-one.

Campbell had crossed over from the outgoing matches and was waiting to pick up the top single between Britain's Ronnie White and Harvie Ward, winner of both US and

Well, *he's* in

British titles and one of the greatest amateur golfers since World War II.

'Having a good game, Junior?' said Campbell, addressing handsome little Harvie.

'Heck, no,' Ward replied, 'it is all even.'

Ward proved the killer with a smile; he pulled away to crush White six and five and end Ronnie's eight-year record of not losing a Walker Cup single.

Amateur golf has few personalities more droll than cosmopolite Harry Bentley, Lancashire born but equally at home at St Andrews, Sunningdale, Royal St George's, Paris or Monte Carlo, and appropriately once captain of the International Golfers' Club.

Harry's presence was felt in British and Continental golf from the early nineteen thirties until the mid-fifties. He won the French Open Amateur championship in both 1931 and 1932. After his second successive victory Harry was asked: 'What are your immediate plans?'

Harry still has a Mancunian accent. Thirty years ago it may have been even more pronounced. This did nothing to stop the twice French champion stating: 'I am going to Paris to address my people.'

After Henry Cotton's first Open Championship victory in 1934 he was favourite almost every time he started. Hoylake in 1936 – Alfred Padgham's year – was no exception. Cotton played superbly but could not set his putter alight.

On the final day that regal golfing figure Raymond Oppenheimer, Henry's friend and contemporary, was acting as chief gallery steward to the very much in contention Cotton, then the magnet of the crowds.

A newcomer to the vast throng was overheard by Raymond to enquire: 'Is Cotton driving well?'

Spontaneously from Oppenheimer came the words: 'Sir, it is impossible to tell whether his drives are finishing on the right half or the left half of the fairway.'

It is impossible to tell whether this story more typifies the wit of Oppenheimer or the majesty of Cotton at that time.

The 1963 Ryder Cup match at Atlanta was the first time I heard an amazing sidelight to the great American Bobby Jones's first victory in the British Open Championship in 1926.

It came from Jones's own lips at a dinner to the British and American teams.

He revealed that he and his chief challenger, Al Watrous, decided during the interval between the third and fourth rounds to seek rest and quiet at the peace of their hotel instead of at the clubhouse.

They laid on a taxi to do so and returned by the same means. They had walked straight from the last green to the waiting cab in their golfing clothes.

When they got back to the Royal Lytham and St Annes clubhouse they found that neither had a badge or documents of any kind identifying them as players.

The gatekeeper was adamant. No badge, no entry. How did he know it was Mr Jones and Mr Watrous?

Time was running short. Jones made up his mind on a course of action. He took Watrous by the arm and led him to the public paying entrance where he handed over two half-crowns. And that is how the men who finished first and second in the championship got on to the course to play their dramatic final round together.

Jones's legendary 175-yard shot from sand at the seventeenth clinched the issue for him.

Amid the sandy wastes of the seventeenth fairway today lies a plaque purporting to mark the spot from which Jones played his ball.

A woman golfer was taken to this spot one day. She said in tones of due solemnity: 'Oh, is this where poor Mr Jones is buried?'

It could be said that the professionals of the modern age are taking over from the candid caddies of yesteryear when it comes to golf humour.

Perhaps it all began with Andrew Kirkaldy. Among the immortal pro's ripostes is that of pipe-smoking Ted Ray, contemporary of Vardon and 1912 Open Champion.

Ray was once asked by an aspiring golfer: 'How can I get more length?'

'Hit it a bloody sight harder, mate,' was Ray's unequivocal answer.

How is this for wit? A gushing female admirer charges up to the very bronzed and healthy looking Dai Rees – incidentally Harry Vardon's long serving successor at the South Herts Club near London – and burst forth: 'Dai, what a simply marvellous tan you have. South of France?' 'No. Just South Herts,' was Ree's succinct reply.

Or this? Scot John Stirling, one of the liveliest-minded professionals, who serves at Meyrick Park, Bournemouth, was telling me once that he came under the spell of the drowsy rhythmical swing of America's Julius Boros, twice US Open Champion, after watching a film of the great man.

'I tried to mould my swing on Julius Boros,' said Stirling. 'I ended up swinging more like Julius Caesar.'

A professional on the receiving end of a classical remark was Peter Thomson while practising one year at St Andrews with his well-known local caddie, Wallace Gillespie.

Gillespie gave Thomson the line at a certain hole. Thomson hit the shot perfectly.

They walked on and came to the ball and it lay between two little pot bunkers with only five yards dividing them.

'You didn't give me much margin,' said Thomson. 'Well, you are the Open Champion, aren't you?' replied Gillespie.

Much of the humour in tournament golf comes from gallery reaction as they faithfully follow the masters.

The spectacular Harry Weetman always brings forth the best of comments.

At the Sonning Club in Berkshire I overheard in the clubhouse one day: 'You know that bush beside the ninth green?'

'Yes.'

'Well, Weetman put his ball in there today. The bush isn't there any more.'

The Americans have a salty turn of golfing language. I once heard one say of Weetman: 'Did you see the size divots Harry Weetman takes? They are as big as beaver pelts.'

I reserve my favourite story about a star professional for the close. It concerns Irishman Fred Daly, the 1947 Open Champion.

Some years later he was playing in a professional tournament near Edinburgh. It was shortly after the victory of Ed Furgol in the American Open. Furgol had become a legend because of this wonderful achievement despite the handicap of having his left arm shorter than his right.

Daly was staying at a hotel near the course where a huge but friendly Great Dane had the run of the house. The knowing dog would stroll into the dining-room and encourage guests to give it titbits. Daly was among those unable to resist the dog's pleas.

The hotel manager saw Fred throwing biscuit on to the floor near the dog. He said: 'He is quite harmless, Mr Daly. You can give it to him in your hand.'

Daly hesitated – then still continued throwing the biscuit.

'No fear. Do you think I want to become the Irish Ed Furgol,' said the cautious Fred.

I have gone all this way relating stories concerning famous people and things that actually happened or were said. I have taken no account of the humours of club golf or the mountains of fiction which deal with the lighter side of the game.

Golf is rich in its humourists. Patrick Campbell, George Houghton, Keith Marshall, Rex Lardner, Ring

Lardner, Stephen Potter and George Nash have all delighted us with their amusing invention, and who is there to equal the heydey of P. G. Wodehouse, who once wrote: 'The least thing upsets him on the links. He misses short putts because of the uproar of the butterflies in the adjoining meadows.'

I am convinced golf is a funny game – in every sense of the word. For every humour I have dredged my memory to recall, I know there are a dozen others which I have forgotten.

From *The Golfer's Bedside Book* (Batsford)

5   Par and the Puritans
George Houghton

The old 'Bets Book' of The Honourable Company of
Edinburgh Golfers tells of the skylarking that went on in
the old days, and this has set me wondering whether the
cleaning up that is sweeping through golf may not be a
curse in disguise. Perhaps some of the fun will go, as it
would from football matches if they prohibited the
throwing of toilet rolls.

The British Professional Golfers' Association and the
similar organization in the United States seem to think
that decorum in golf must be preserved at all costs. Fines
are being smacked on the professionals if they are guilty
of any misdemeanour listed in a wide range. No doubt
noble intentions are behind the idea, but some of us
believe that if punishments are needed in golf then the
wrong kind of people are being admitted. On the other
hand, one might say that if our great game is primarily
for participants, who is to decide how we should partici-
pate?

Golfers who have given the matter thought are now
considering if players are being punished for the wrong
kind of sins. Surely the yardstick must be whether or not

the culprit is guilty of doing anything detrimental to anyone's enjoyment.

Cleaning up golf is not new, but in the old days these
matters were dealt with more gracefully.

The following entry was made in an ancient golf
record: 'Leith, 1776. This day Lieutenant James Daly-
rymple, of the 43rd Regiment, being convicted of playing five different times at Golf without his uniform, was
fined Six Pints (of claret), having confessed the heinous-
ness of his crime'. A footnote states ' At his own request
he was fined Three Pints more '.

Another item concerns a William Wood, who, having
won the Gold Medal, had some of the gilt erased from
the ginger bread by suffering a fine of two tappit hens
for appearing on the links without his red coat.

I doubt whether anyone else is affected by how a
player dresses, but I suppose rules are rules, and the
oldies were sticklers for appearance. There were other
punishable offences. For example, Club Captains at St
Andrews during the latter part of the eighteenth century
had to pay fines of two pints of claret for every meeting
missed. It was important, it seems, that club meetings
should be attended, and the member who carelessly had
a private party and invited other golfers on a club night
was stiffly fined a magnum of claret; additionally, each
absentee had to produce a bottle.

Fines in claret were such a good idea, and because
the tipple was always consumed 'at the scene of the
crime' any unpleasantness was soon washed away. Instead
of being put in the doghouse for his misdemeanour, the

guilty party would be exonerated by members in much too generous a mood to bear rancour.

Nowadays, the system of fines is brutal and confusing. The trouble seems to be commercialism. The sponsors and cash customers must be kept happy at any price. Well, if the organizers of professional golf in the nineteen seventies think that their department needs cleaning up, no doubt it does.

Unless he was hit, no one minded when American golfer Tommy Bolt flung a club into a crowd after fluffing a shot. In fact, before he mellowed, hundreds of spectators went to tournaments solely to see the tantrums of old 'Thunderbolt'.

Mr Bolt would be heavily fined these days, in cash not claret. Officials at the professional tournaments are furnished with a crime list, indicating appropriate fines. Throwing clubs costs money, so does 'Criticism of the course' because this not only upsets the club but also the sponsor who is putting up the cash prizes. In the USA, course criticism could result in the outspoken player handing over 150 dollars, which is what happened in an Open Championship when a competitor loudly declared that it would take only a dozen bulldozers to make the Chaska course into a useful housing estate.

Other 'crimes' are slow play, bad manners, late on the tee, and foul language. Mercifully, the word 'foul' is used, so presumably golfers can carry on with their normal 'bad' language without penalty.

Twelve offences are punishable. Surprisingly, that which some people consider to be the most serious thing

A very tricky course . . .

that can happen on any golf course is not even mentioned.

I am referring to cheating.

Perhaps the governing bodies consider that the Rules of Golf adequately cover the neat art. They don't. Thank heaven this jolly way of gaining ascendancy over a friendly opponent will always be alive and kicking, because most golfers refuse to be slaves to rules.

Genial cheaters, who seldom bet more than a ball on a match but passionately love golf's cosy rivalry, hate reforms and such like. They believe that golf is too good to be messed about. Particularly, we dread the prospect of the game being soured by puritans.

A man whose title could be set to music, Commissioner of the Tournament Players' Division of the American Professional Golfers' Association, delivered his own Gettysburg address: 'The opportunities to cheat and take unfair advantage are plentiful. Our biggest safeguard is personal integrity. Golf, from its very beginning, has been a gentleman's game ...'

On the same theme, a British official actually used these words: 'Serious safeguards must be taken immediately if the game is to remain pure'.

Pure? PURE? Bless my soul! What are they trying to do to us?

If this out-of-place puritanism is only to apply to professionals, okay. Let them clean up their business and run it as honestly as they like, but the happy hackers, the mid-week knock-abouts, the cheery cheats, the game's mainstays ... want golf exactly as it is and has been for hundreds of years – nice and naughty.

What about this 1815 entry in the Edinburgh records of the Bruntsfield Links: 'Mr Scott betted One Guinea with Mr M'Dowall that he would drive a ball from the Golf House, Bruntsfield Links, over Arthur Seat, at 45 strokes. Mr Scott lost. Mr Brown betted with Mr Spalding one gallon of whisky that he would drive a ball over Arthur Seat on the same terms and at the same number of strokes as the above bet. Mr Spalding lost, as Mr Brown drove his ball over Arthur Seat in 44 strokes.'

I suppose the purifiers would have suppressed that kind of lark.

Any attempt to chase fun from golf should be resisted, but even reforms would be bearable if the fines were in claret. This seems to have been the golfers' favourite tipple in the old days, and for a wager, singing Jamie Balfour, Secretary of The Honourable Company of Edinburgh Golfers, drank a glass of claret on each tee while playing twelve holes at Leith.

Of course, skylarking in golf has not always involved claret. Often just high spirits, as when two members of Radyr played a harassing cross-country match to Porthcawl in the nineteen sixties; from Pyecombe a similar long distance whack ended at Royal Eastbourne, fifteen miles away.

Always there have been frolics to add spice to golf, and take the sadness from missing yard putts.

No one in his sober senses (at least in public) will deplore a swing to honesty, yet, let's face it, even cheating can be amusing. To some extent, we all have a go. Even the fair sex.

To gain advantage over opponents, women employ their own special tricks. Verbal distractions are ineffective, because lady golfers are immune to chatter. Inhuman inventiveness – like pretending accidentally to drop a photograph of an opponent's husband – is regularly practised to gain advantage in these unholy combats.

Male or female golfers know that worry is the big killer. A rapier thrust is not necessary to pierce the heart. You can do it with a hat pin. Advantage can be gained by wearing a colour-clashing pullover – if you are matched against an artist ... The man with a chatterbox reputation never uttered a word for sixteen holes, and won his match because the opponent was distracted by the abnormal silence.

An under-cover publisher – distributing in plain sealed envelopes to a limited number of well-scattered subscribers – should issue a small book of hints on cheating honestly. If such a boon ever came to golfdom it would be regarded as a joke, but the tricks would be tried.

A man with his back to the wall can utter a casual sentence which will send his opponent crashing. The object is to get your adversary thinking, preferably about his swing. The brain bubbles like boiling porridge; the result is confusion and a savage slice. Strange that the purists, trying so hard to tame golf, have overlooked the gentle art of cheating.

One must be thankful for small mercies, nevertheless, there are many objectionable areas to which the cleaners-

Do be more careful! – You might have hit me!

up could direct their attention. Particular cad-categories come to mind where stiff fines would be justified.

When a sadistic lout says 'I'll see it in', making you hole out a two-foot tiddler putt which any decent golfer would concede, that lout deserves to suffer because he himself has caused suffering.

That great amateur golfer Doctor Tweddell stopped playing top tournaments and said, 'Why should I worry myself sick trying to hole yard putts when I can play with friends who will give me that length?'

This is a good example, and one can only repeat that a guide for imposing punishments in golf might be the irritations which spoil the pleasure of others.

For example: a trouser tucker-in who carries a bag of nondescript clubs, and hits his tired old ball thirty yards further than you can smite yours, surely deserves to be dealt with severely. He has wounded your pride, and in golf this is important. The outsider could be denied the use of the course until he either looks like a golfer or doesn't play so well.

The most offensive and damaging aspects of golf are often unapparent to non-players. How can an outsider know the suffering in a golfer's breast when an opponent asks for a tee? A little plastic tee! The cheapest thing in golf. No one minds giving one, but this time it is different. The adversaries are driving off at the first hole in a knock-out competition. One of the players is so *unworried* that he has not even bothered to check his equipment! That man's careless confidence is a match-winning factor. He should be punished for taking unfair advantage.

Another type of offender who gets away with it too often is the scourge who, at the end of a match which he lost, pays the wager with a shabby golf ball. Instead of being encased in a lovely glistening wrapper, the paper is smooth with handling and the print is rubbed. Clearly the ball has been handed on and on as currency in many matches before yours. The golfer who does not pay out with a brand new ball, fresh and virginal, should be reprimanded. Victory deserves its full reward.

The opponent who tells you what you are doing wrong should be fined. Even if his diagnosis is correct, the advice adds nothing to the enjoyment of the game. The fact that we are nearly all hint-givers is no excuse, and extenuating circumstances should not (repeat 'not') be taken into account. The man with whom you are playing makes his fourth successive bad shot. 'For heaven's sake,' he howls, 'what am I doing wrong?' At a moment like this, there are two alternatives. First, you can deliver a long and most enjoyable (for you) lecture. Or you can sadly shake your head, indicating that the man's predicament is one of life's great mysteries. Although by keeping quiet you are making a sacrifice, the latter is the right course of action. When a golfer asks you to tell him what he is doing wrong, the last thing he wants is to know.

Quite clearly, professionals enjoy giving lessons. It is such fun to see what happens when you tell someone to 'hit more against the left hip'. But for we amateur hackers golf must never be selfish, so at all times mum's the word.

A horrible thought, but fines may come into amateur golf whether we like it or not. Probably a voluntary system of self-imposed penalties would be best. Without doubt, the main offence would be 'foul' language, and most of us would fairly happily slip our two-bob-a-cuss debts into a box in the locker-room – *if the cash could be used for course maintenance.*

Golf would be a costly affair for the majority, but I would hate to know that certain miserable, blameless members would pay nothing into the fines box. They would get free benefits! Is not this in itself a major misdemeanour?

Considering all aspects, and to be strictly fair, I would like to propose that the puritans should be fined, and the rank and file go scot free.

6 Liberty, Sorority, Equality!

Henry Longhurst

It appears that in my recent absence abroad a number of letters reached this office from frustrated ladies deploring their continued lowly status in the local golf club. Members of Parliament are only too familiar with the barrage of postal protests which arrive simultaneously from all parts of the country, every letter by a singular coincidence couched in identical terms, and I am sure that all Hon and Rt Hon Gentlemen, as they cast them into the wastepaper basket, spare a sympathetic thought for the diligence with which the writers sat down and copied out the circular.

In the present case the variety of expression suggests no such collusion and the Ladies' Golf Unions are hereby acquitted of being the spider in a sinister web of propaganda. It seems that a great many women golfers do indeed feel sore at not being allowed to play on Sundays and at being kept in a separate tent, as it were, like the female Bedouin Arab. The spirit of revolt seethes throughout the land. At any moment we shall find a couple of golfing Pankhursts chained to the railings of the Royal and Ancient, and I only hope I am there to see it.

The truth is that women golfers have never, in this country at least, been taken with a seriousness which they do not deserve. In America the sight of Miss Patty Berg running a couple of miles every morning in a track suit to strengthen her legs for golf excites nothing but admiration – though tinged in my own case by the thought that it brought her last year in prize money alone rather more than the salary of a British Cabinet Minister. Here at home such a spectacle would excite that uneasy mixture of respect and regret which so many of us experience at the circus.

The cross which women golfers in this country have to bear is not so much that they cannot play on Sundays – though I dare say a good many clubs would let them if they paid the same subscription as the men – but that, like mothers-in-law, they are the butt of innumerable jokes, most of them as feeble as the one about practising for the mixed foursomes. Furthermore, it is assumed by those who know no better that they (*a*) habitually cheat, and (*b*) are possessed of what a colleague of mine once described as 'billiard table legs, leathery faces, and clumsy great paws'. You have only to look at the golfing girls of today to see that at least the latter charge is grossly unfair.

Having most of my life been a rabid segregationist, I have now mellowed – or ratted, whichever way you like to look at it – into an equally rabid integrationist. I like to see the sexes intermingle in the clubhouse. I think the

Okay, okay! – *Don't* take my advice

time has passed when the ladies on a Sunday morning should go in by a separate entrance and be confined to a small back room, there to engage in outward pleasantries and dark inward thoughts, tapping their tiny feet while they pluck up courage to send a message through to the lord and master – whose own finest hour with his witty friends is being spoiled, if they only knew it, by the call of conscience and covert glances to see if the steward is approaching with the dread summons.

It may perhaps be no coincidence that three of the happiest clubs I know have only one main room and the question of apartheid therefore does not arise, but this, of course, is every club's domestic affair and only becomes anyone else's business when a championship or some such is played on its course. In this case I do solemnly declare that any club unwilling to open wide its portals on that occasion should, with suitable thanks and regret, decline the championship.

To come 6,000 miles to play in a British championship, as some of our Dominions and American friends do, and find that your wife cannot meet you in the clubhouse is surely no longer to be endured.

All moralists, however, feel entitled to make what I believe Charles I called 'mental reservations' in their own favour and in this instance I unhesitatingly make one in mine, namely the holy of holies at St Andrews, where, in any case, there are a women's club and plenty of hotels adjacent to the eighteenth green. As it would be improper for me to comment upon the internal affairs of the R. and A., I content myself with quoting the words of a senior member twenty-odd years ago on observing for the first time a woman cashier in the dining-room.

'Damn it,' he said, 'it's a woman. Last woman I saw in here was an American. She was smoking. In the silence room. I soon had 'er out.'

Long may such stalwarts live to defend this particular citadel. As to the others, let the gates be thrown open and the barricades unmanned. Liberty, sorority, equality!

From *Always On Sunday* (Cassell)

7   The Golf Course
Michael Green

There are grave doubts as to whether golf can count as a branch of Coarse Sport. For in golf there is an invisible barrier between those who can and those who can't. It is not a game with the infinitely subtle variations of in-efficiency that exist in other sports.

Rugby players vary from the dashing international who can run fifty yards with three broken ribs, to the weedy, undersized threequarter of the seventh team who can't run five yards without resting, but the Rugby Union still recognizes the existence of both types and legislates for them. The MCC legislate for both test matches and village green cricket.

But this does not apply to golf. It is true there is a difference between those who are scratch and those who have a handicap of twenty-four, but beneath these there is a vast army of players who are not good enough to have a handicap at all and who, therefore, according to the authorities of the game, do not exist.

I am one of the invisible golfers, part of the shadow battalions which may be seen hacking their way round

any course, their progress marked by flying clods of earth
and despairing oaths.

One of the difficulties of golf is that unlike the position
in other sports, one does not get better with coaching.
Why do golf professionals drive about in Rolls-Royces?
Because their coaching never works. If you go to a professional to be cured of a slice he will do it at a cost of
some five pounds. The unhappy golfer will then be left
with a hook instead.

If a professional's coaching worked he would run out
of customers, instead of which the country is full of
unhappy people chained to their golf professional as a
neurotic is chained to his favourite psychiatrist.

Neither can a Coarse Sportsman take advantage of his
age or his opponent's infirmities to win. I have been
thoroughly beaten by a man with two wooden legs who
drove round in a wheel chair, and the biggest thrashing
of my life came from a charming old chap who an-
nounced that he had taken a stroke for every year of his
age. He went round in ninety-two.

All a Coarse Golfer can do is to resign himself to his
fate and try to alleviate it by various wheezes. Note that
a Coarse Sportsman is usually too bad to win at golf by
using trickery. One might win at cricket by altering the
pavilion clock, or at rugby by kicking the ball into the
canal, but in golf it isn't really much use sneezing and
making your opponent miss a putt if you yourself are
then going to take four more strokes to put the wretched
ball down.

A Coarse Golfer can only concentrate on saving his face.

My own method is to play with a serious expression, a on-with-the-motley look that suggests heavy suffering underneath. After my opponent has holed out to win I shake him by the hand firmly, and say quietly, 'Well, she was a good wife to me.'

I then walk swiftly away shaking my head, and muttering, 'In the midst of life . . .'

This can only be used once with the same opponent, of course, but a Coarse Golfer will find that he will not usually have the same opponent more than once, unless it is someone of his own standard.

I often wonder whether I wouldn't be better at golf if I changed my clubs.

They were bought in a little junk *boutique* near Hammersmith. They are wooden-shafted and came in a thin tubular bag which folds up like a concertina when stood upright. Strange oaths like Mashie Niblick are engraved on the face of the clubs. For a long time I imagined they must have belonged to an eccentric Scots millionaire, old Mashie Niblick, living up at St Andrews on tea and toast ('Aye, Meestair Niblick, 'twas a fine idea to engrave your name on yon wee club . . .').

The first club is my putter. It is a malignant little stick with a great bulbous lump of lead on one end, as if it had goitre. As a putter it is supremely useless, but I frequently drive with it in moments of desperation. Then comes a strange device which has no name visible on the face.

When standing upright it looks like a musical note, so I call it my crotchet.

It is the only club in the bag which has any warmth or

spark of life. There is a strange bond between us. I could swear it talks to me, begging for its life as I am about to snap it across my knee after sending my last ball through a local bus.

It is, of course, wooden-shafted like the rest of them. Wooden-shafted clubs have this supreme advantage that they can be snapped in moments of uncontrollable rage such as are common to all golfers. I remember seeing an elderly golfer seriously injured while trying to snap his putter, forgetting that it was steel-shafted. The end sprang back and felled him to the ground.

Now come two clubs which I shall not discuss, including the revolting Mashie Niblick. We have nothing in common. They are malignant creatures, yet they will not leave me. I threw them into a spinney once, and a little boy brought them back, so I had to give him sixpence. I hurled them into the water hole, and they floated, I gave them away and the recipient gave them back next day. They would not even burn.

Finally there is my driver. I do not use this merely for driving. By some strange alchemy, it is better on the green than my putter (which is better off the tee). But in many ways it is the most interesting of all my clubs, since I never use it without something sensational happening.

I used it for my first stroke in golf.

It was a Sunday morning and there was a long queue behind us as I teed up in front of the clubhouse, addressed the ball, waggled the clubhead, put the ball back on the tee, swung the club in a vast arc round my waist, and lashed out.

An interesting shot, provided his braces stand the strain

A huge clod of earth vanished down the fairway.

Behind me there was a low moan, as of golfers in pain.

'Practice,' I muttered cheerfully and swung again.

This time there was a clicking noise and the ball vanished. My eyes strained to follow a little dot hurtling away towards the green. It was the clubhead, followed by two hundred yards of twine.

A shout drew my attention and I looked up, to see a member standing at right angles to me fling up his arms and fall senseless to the ground.

'Good God,' said a stout man in plus-fours who was watching. 'He's going to kill us all.'

My opponent, who was a solicitor, stepped forward and laid a tender hand on my arm.

'Remember that you aren't obliged to say anything, old fellow,' he whispered. 'You aren't forced to make a statement or even apologize, if that could be construed as an admission of guilt.'

Fortunately an apology would have been useless. The member was unconscious. He was carried supine into the clubhouse with a Dunlop 65 embedded in his ear, and we continued the round. It seemed the only decent thing to do.

After all this it may be rather surprising to learn that I have had the pleasure of the greatest experience a Coarse Golfer, or indeed any other golfer, can undergo. I refer, of course, to the occasion on which I holed in one.

It wasn't any of those puny holes-in-one that third-rate professionals manage on a two-hundred-yard hole, with the pin nestling in the hollow of a cup-shaped green thirty feet across. No, this was the real thing. A hole-in-one on a five hundred and sixty-six yard hole, par five and uphill.

I drove into the teeth of a fierce wind. I was playing against my great friend Askew, and the wind was so strong that when he drove, the ball shot vertically upwards and landed behind him in the middle of a foursome who were patiently waiting for us to get on with it.

It was not perhaps one of my best drives. I have a natural slice, like so many of the greatest golfers, and normally I allow for this by aiming at an angle of forty-five degrees to the hole. Unfortunately I hit this ball quite straight, with the result that aided by the wind it disappeared in a great arc, somewhere over my shoulder.

Then Fate took a hand. Lurking furtively to one side of the fairway, surrounded by gorse and heather, was a small sewer pipe. My ball struck this object, rebounded into the next fairway, trickled on to the green and after a moment's agonizing indecision, elected to go down the hole.

I thus became the first player on that course to hole on the sixteenth green after driving from the seventh tee. I also became the first player in the history of the game to perform a hole-in-one off a public sewer.

From *The Art Of Coarse Sport* (Hutchinson)

8 The Perils of Broadcasting

Tom Scott

'Over to Tom Scott ...' These words which have been heard on the air many, many times, I'm glad to say were first heard during the Open Championship at Royal Portrush in 1951.

A memorable championship, not because of my broadcasting debut, but for the fact that it was won by a British golfer, Max Faulkner. I was to wait eighteen years before I broadcast the news of another British victory but that is another story, and one which has been written about a great deal. I refer to Tony Jacklin's victory in 1969.

How did I start in broadcasting? More by chance than anything else. I was in the Nineteenth Club in London one day at lunchtime (must have had more money in those days) and was speaking to Henry Longhurst who was then doing radio work for the BBC, but who later graduated to television to become the world's No. 1 TV golf commentator. Henry was just leaving the club when he suddenly turned to me and said, 'How would you like to do some broadcasting from the Open at Portrush?'

'Broadcasting? Me? I don't know,' I exclaimed. 'What will I have to do?'

'Well,' replied Henry. 'I'm going to be a link man in the clubhouse and there're going to be two chaps in little towers out on the course. I'll be in communication with them and all they have to do is to speak into the microphone and say what's going on.'

'All right, I'll have a go at it,' I replied. And that's how it all started. But mind you it nearly finished before it began, so to speak, for in those days the only way you could get scores out on the course was to obtain the services of a small boy to ask the players how they were standing, write the scores on a piece of paper and hand them to me up in the tower. I had engaged a boy at half a crown a day (out of my own pocket) and when I was on the air for the first time I saw the boy coming tearing towards the little tower. I was describing his breathless progress to the listeners – filling in time really – when suddenly he fell tip over elbow. I blurted out, ' The little So and So has fallen flat on his face. Wait a minute and I'll go and get the scores.' And I did, leaving the microphone all by itself. Fortunately everybody seemed to think it was funny or my career as a radio commentator might have been strangled at birth.

Now I have tallied up somewhere around two thousand broadcasts, all of them on golf, the shortest of them a few seconds, the longest about half an hour, and it's all been the greatest fun, except of course for the times when things have gone wrong, and in two thousand times things have gone wrong sometimes. I remember being on a sports programme on a Saturday night when commentators in Brighton, Oxford, and two or three other places not far from London were all 'lost' so to speak – I mean the studio in London was unable to contact them.

In desperation the announcer said: 'Well, the only thing I can do is to see if we can get Cape Town, and there's not much chance of that with all this technical trouble. Cape Town are you listening?' Back came the reply at once loud and clear. 'Yes, Cape Town here ... and in the second test match ...'

But it's not fair to mention technical troubles because the BBC engineers are marvellous and I never cease to wonder at their skill in linking up the various outside broadcast points. Mishaps are rare.

I do remember a mishap of my own making, though. There are two types of microphones, one which is on a fixed stand in front of you and the other, a hand microphone, which you pick up and hold against your mouth. On one occasion I was using a stand mike and then had to change over to the other one, for some reason or another. And I started my broadcast but forgot to pick up the hand mike. The listeners missed the first few words, in fact all the words before I had regained my senses. At the end of the broadcast the announcer apologized for listeners missing the first few words because of what was 'obviously a technical hitch'.

For a long time I invariably hit my head on the top of the doorway when I was going into a mobile broadcasting

– And stop worrying about your golf! – get to the office more often, and *RELAX*

hut. The doors are not really very high and time after time I banged my head. Fortunately I got off with nothing worse than the odd cut, and a sore head the next day, thus being much luckier than the unfortunate football commentator in Rome who was concussed in a car crash on his way to the stadium. He carried on and did his commentary although remembering little or nothing about it afterwards. That was a heroic effort.

Now even the green hut used for golf broadcasts is being used less and less and usually now there is a finely equipped caravan sometimes with two studios, an office and a fully fitted out technical department. A bit different from the chicken house, or was it a pigeon loft, I was once working from. The stench was a bit off-putting but not so off-putting as birds flying around attending to the needs of nature from time to time.

And talking of birds, I once did a day's broadcasting in a little room off the ladies' locker quarters at a well-known club. Every time I wanted to get to the microphone I had to pass through the locker-room. Once I dashed in and there standing in front of me was a lady wearing nothing but bra and pants. I apologized hurriedly and she said airily, 'Oh don't mind me, I'm the lady captain'. (I never really have discovered why I should not mind because she was the lady captain, except that it could be lady captains have certain privileges in a golf club. No it can't be that. That would never do. No club would ever let the lady captain run round in her underwear.)

After the day's work was done I was having a drink at

the bar and was joined by a man whom I did not know very well although I did know he was a member of the club. He asked me where I had been broadcasting from and I told him in a room off the ladies' locker-room. 'And do you know,' I said, 'I bet I've seen something you've never seen.'

'What's that?' he enquired.

'The lady captain in her bra and pants,' I replied.

He looked straight at me for a moment and then grinned. 'Oh yes I have,' he answered. 'I've been married to her for fifteen years.'

And to make matters worse the lady captain came up at that very moment and asked what we were laughing about. Fortunately she had a sense of humour as well as her husband.

Of course listeners love to hear commentators make a proper botch of something. It really makes their day. If I've said something I shouldn't have said I can be sure some friends, and some strangers too, will ring up and say: 'You said on Saturday that Harry Vardon won his last Open championship in 1913 and he didn't. He won it in 1914.' Or: 'You said Palmer's score at Troon was 275, it was 276.'

Naturally these mistakes are either caused by slips of the tongue or my not being able to read my notes. Every commentator likes to feel that he does his homework properly. But everybody's human, after all. Then, of course, there is the pronunciation of unusual names such as Hsieh Yung Yo, Kogelmuller, Le Grange, Gallardo, and lots of others. I had a good few goes at Hsieh before

I got hold of him and asked him how to pronounce his name, and the pronunciation was very simple really, 'Shay', it was. For Le Grange, when I am on a British programme I say Le Grange as it is written, but when I am on a world service programme I give him the guttural South African pronunciation, which is something like Le Hraunshe. Being a Scot I can make a pretty good stab at this, although I don't say I've got it right. I give Gollardo the same treatment. 'Gallardo' if I'm on a British programme but Guyardo if I'm on a world service programme. Again I may not have got it right but it's a step in the right direction, I feel, and shows overseas listeners that you're trying.

Interviews are often fun to do because most golfers are very good with overseas ones, tops in the main, but not altogether. Tony Jacklin is great to interview because he just asks 'What do you want me to say?' and when you make a few suggestions to him off he goes.

The very last one I did with Tony was after the Wills Tournament at Dalmahoy and he was in great form, such great form that he had mentioned the make of his golf clubs, his golf balls, and his car. There was no point in stopping him although he was inadvertently advertising the products he was using. It would have ruined the whole interview so I just let him go on. A jolly good interview it was too.

Jack Nicklaus is good, and Gary Player can always come across with some story about keeping fit or on his latest hobby horse whatever that may be. And Lee Trevino is always good for a laugh.

Shall we do the full 18, or stop when I reach 300?

The first time I interviewed him I said to him, 'That manager of yours is a pretty big fellow'.

'Big fellow,' replied Lee. 'I should say he is. Before he became my manager he weighed a hundred and forty pounds. Now he weighs a hundred and ninety and going up all the time.' Just a joke, but funny the first time.

Another Trevino story.

'Lee, are you a Mexican or an American?'

'Well I used to be a Mexican, that was when I was poor. But now I'm rich I'm an American. Whoever heard of a rich Mexican?'

The thing is of course that golfers are mostly always good to interview, because in the main the time you want to interview them is after they have won. But I have interviewed a few losers, and I must say that of them Dai Rees was the best. I interviewed him after he had so narrowly lost the open championship at Royal Birkdale in 1961 and he amazed me how composed he was at what must have been the biggest disappointment of his life. For myself I should have just wanted to crawl into a corner and be on my own. But to Dai's eternal credit he put a very brave face on things indeed, although he must have been feeling like death.

In all the years I have been broadcasting never has any golfer refused to be interviewed, although I must admit that one or two have kept me waiting a long time. I've also interviewed quite a number of caddies who are very good value indeed. But some of them are at great pains to disguise their identity, to make it shall we say just a little more difficult for the income tax man to contact them. They have plenty of stories to tell but most of them, alas, are unfit for the radio, but at the rate the theatre and television are going on, we shall soon be able to have caddies tell stories without them bringing a blush to the cheeks of a single listener, or a married one either if it comes to that.

Yes, it's a lot of fun broadcasting, but it has its problems too, such as the time I was going from Lindrick to Nottingham for a broadcast. I can't quite remember the distance but it's well over twenty miles, and I had left myself very short of time, for not only did I have to get to Nottingham, but had to get to the studio, and although I had the address I had never been to Nottingham before. I drove like mad and got to the centre of Nottingham. The problem was now to find the street in which the studio was situated. I drove along the kerb slowly waiting until I could spot a really intelligent face. I spotted what I thought was one and stopped, handing him the slip of paper, only to be told he couldn't read or write. I didn't think in that case he would be able to give me concise directions so I drove on eventually to stop again. In this instance I am sorry to say that the young man I asked was mentally retarded. Now in desperation I stopped a young lady who, mistaking my intentions, immediately started to get into the car. That had to be stopped pretty smartly (I had read about girls in Nottingham) so I drove on again and mercifully I came upon a policeman, so all was well. I arrived at the studio with just a few minutes to spare.

Yes, in thinking things over I think that one of the

necessities of life for radio commentators is a sense of humour. It could be, of course, that their radio listeners need a sense of humour as well.

9 The Common Touch
Steve Roberts

We noticed it first as we approached the first green. That rustling in the long grass in the shade of the tree to the right. It was a hot August Bank Holiday. 'I hope that's not a snake,' I said.

'Of course not,' replied my partner. 'It's nothing to worry about. In fact it would be better if you ignored it.'

Indeed it would. For the cause of the activity was a couple obviously in love and oblivious to everything else as they proved their compatibility and virility.

'A member?' I joked. 'No. I've never seen the chap before,' he replied. 'But we can't do anything about it,' he added. 'You see, although this is a private club this is common land -- and it seems anyone can wander around and do anything they like.'

In spite of all my efforts to remember that one of Arnold Palmer's four 'C's' for success is Concentration, I could not rid my mind completely of the other game going on at the greenside or keep my head down and eye on the ball for that matter. Three putts against my opponent's two put me one hole down straight away.

Local knowledge of the unusual distractions likely on this course was going to be worth more than the customary two shots my opponent was granting me. As I very soon found out. A shot a hole would not have been too generous in view of what followed.

At the very next hole I stood proudly watching one of my better drives finish 250 yards (or thereabouts, I reckon) in the middle of the fairway. My opponent hooked his badly. 'Now I'll square matters,' I thought.

What optimism! As I strode towards my ball a much larger oblong ball sailed across the fairway, landed full toss beside my ball and sent it scurrying into the rough. Surely I wasn't having hallucinations. The sun wasn't that hot. But I got even hotter as I watched a horde of screeching young schoolboys, resplendent in bright red jerseys, chasing after their ball.

'Getoutofit,' I yelled. What a time and place to practise for next term's rugby. And when I eventually found my ball trampled by the fleeing feet deep in the rough I longed to scrum down with the young villains. Although, on reflection, maybe not on my own.

I replaced my ball as near as possible to its original spot but my watering eyes and shaky swing resulted in an atrocious second shot, and a little better third. Meanwhile the opposition, while expressing sympathy in words, showed little in action as he hacked his ball into the clear and pitched it on for one putt and another win. Two down after two holes. This was ridiculous.

Just a few deep breaths and I'll be my normal steady par playing self. Whatever else happens I'm not going to

Making a hole where your drive finishes may simplify the game, but it isn't golf

be put off. It was just a bit of bad luck. After all it's only a game. Still, it would be nice to win for the sake of the club. The thoughts galloped through my head as we trollied our way to the third tee.

A dog leg to the right. Great. So long as that slice of mine doesn't happen too soon I might even get round the bend with a long 'un. And everything is under control now. The fairway was clear, wide and sunny. I felt almost pleased when my partner cracked one down the middle. He might not be able to see the green from there but, after all, I was not yet wishing to beat him because of his bad shots. I felt I could better that one – and did. It was a scorcher just beyond the bend.

But as I went forward to make my next shot I nearly went round the bend, figuratively. For, in between us and the green, a cricket match was taking place. Two sets of stumps, men with bats, widely placed fielders ... the lot. Admittedly the players were not properly dressed, one or two actually had their braces showing. And I don't suppose there were more than eight of them. But to me they looked hordes. Shouts of 'fore' did little more than annoy the two scampering between the wickets, assuming the waving of their bats was for the same reason I was energetically signalling with my club.

We had quite a heated argument as to who was interfering with whose game before they decided to let us play on. And they demonstrated even more their lack of knowledge of correct golf course behaviour as we tried to proceed with dignity. Even Tony Jacklin could not have avoided a similar topped shot had his ears been assailed as mine were. At least, so I attempted to console myself.

So I lost another hole for my opponent appeared un-moved by all this. Although I thought I sensed a spot of embarrassment when one of the cricketers called, 'Hello George, enjoying yourself?'

I was beginning to lose heart. It must be a conspiracy. The home club must arrange all these distractions when they are playing a match against unsuspecting strangers. But no one could be blamed for the incident at the next hole. This should have been a dog leg in view of what happened.

For the first time we did not see a soul. I felt the tension unwinding as we strolled along. I began talking again in friendly fashion. That choked feeling in my throat had gone. Yes, this was wonderful weather for a walk even if the golf was not so good.

But also walking in our vicinity unbeknown to us was a pack of dogs. And as we approached the green they dashed out of the shrubs into full view. We stood awhile before making our approach shots in order to let the happy, barking throng cross to the trees the other side. Then we stood astounded as one large black-and-white mongrel stopped suddenly on the front edge of the green; judging from his attitude, he must have been watching the cricket match earlier. For he poised himself perfectly in a wicket-keeping position.

Yes, you've guessed it. My perfect chip, dead on line for the pin, stopped dead as it pitched plonk on the canine 'visiting card'. 'It's turned out nice again,' quipped my opponent. I was speechless. And if balls did not cost six·shillings a time I would have left it poised there as a memorial.

For that was literally the sticky end to my hopes of ever winning this match.. My day was ruined. Still, the true sportsman always plays on regardless. It's difficult to disregard the fact that being four down after four holes needs a remarkable recovery, but it can be done. I remembered all the remarkable come-backs from 'impossible' positions. But the stars never experienced such excremental difficulties.

So I played on, tight-lipped. I never have had much of a stomach for clearing up after non-house-trained dogs, even little puppies. This really was a test of character as well as golf. Keep your cool, I kept repeating to myself. After all George – yes, I outwardly maintained a friendly attitude – had no control over that dog. Any more than I had. For my viciously thrown No. 9 iron missed his backside by a mile.

The dogs had disappeared as we stood on the fifth tee. The yelping had faded out of earshot. In perfect peace George hit his No. 5 iron bang on to the green. I'm longer than he is, so a six will do, I reckoned. But I reckoned without the next episode in my day of dismay.

I carefully checked on the position of the feet, the hands, and the rest of the golfing musts and was just about to let fly when rustling in the undergrowth and muttered voices caused me to halt. And into view, and right by the tee, came our two lovers. This time they

That makes 65 flukes, one after the other!

were merely holding hands. But they had more to say.

They stopped and did keep quiet when I made my shot but I knew before my ball plopped into a bunker that another hole was lost. Six down. My eyes became as misty as those of the happy twosome. And I'm sure I felt even more exhausted.

The seventh hole would have been navigated successfully enough if that stupid woman had not told that stupid little boy to 'stand still and watch this clever man hit the ball into the hole'. From 100 yards mark you!

And at the eighth there was a chance of at least a half when I was on the green in two, the same as George, and nearer the hole.

But however did he manage to get down in two putts while I took five? I think he must have been deaf. For every time we went to take a putt a group of louts lying on the grass with their heads sticking up over the edge of the green made rude noises.

My initial attempt to scare them away by indulging in even ruder shouting and brandishing a club ended immediately they stood up and threatened, 'Well, whatchergoing to do about it mate?' For they were all strapping six footers.

As we passed the family of picnickers half-way down the ninth – two scruffy little boys actually had buckets and spades in a bunker – all my thoughts of ever finishing the course had vanished. Nine down at the turn, one more hole would see the end of my agony.

But I discovered it was only a nine holes course. As George led the way towards the first tee again visions of lovers, cricketers, dogs and the rest flashed before my eyes.

My head whirled. 'Sorry George,' I said, 'I can't stand any more. I concede the match. Well played. After all you only needed ...'

Eventually I stopped mumbling and stumbled back towards the clubhouse. My only thought was to get away as soon as possible and back to the peace of my own privately owned club and course before I threw away my clubs and gave up the game.

As I went to the car park a couple of lads came up offering to sell me some balls cheaply – one looked suspiciously like one I'd lost along the torturous track.

'Goodbye,' called George, 'Come again some time' – and he wasn't joking.

If this misadventure sounds unreal I can assure you that I have embellished the facts only slightly. For the sake of the club I am not giving its name. But if any of you are invited to play at a course on common land I suggest you don't go on an August Bank Holiday.

10 By the Right, Dress!
Robert Anderson

The old Army command is certainly not one that applies in any context to the average golfer. There is nothing uniform about the weird and wonderful sartorial approach to the game by the club member. Nowadays, the tendency is for the golfer to adopt the sort of colourful fashions that would do credit to the latest Paris collections. In other words the player who thrashes his way round the course on a Sunday morning seems to be convinced that whatever his standard of play, he will not be outshone in elegance by his most experienced opponent.

To appreciate this desire to look good, however, one has to regard the average golfer in the same way as one contemplates the emergence of a butterfly from its cocoon. For golf and golfers' dress is a very seasonable business. Think of the determined all-the-year-round enthusiast, who will play in all weathers: rain, frost, snow and even fog, and you will appreciate that he must adopt his garb to the seasons of the golfing year.

Let us start in January when the temperature is near freezing point and it would be a sin even to take the dog for a walk. Yet in these conditions, the golfer must have his game and he has to dress accordingly. It is no exaggeration to say that throughout these winter months the question of how to dress is one that taxes the ingenuity. Many golfers settle for a cap, corduroys and three heavy pullovers. But there are others, who will do anything to go one better than their fellow members and achieve the aim of all winter golfers to keep warm and snug throughout the game. So what do we get? There are golfers who play in anoraks, more suitably clad for Everest than the links. There are others who favour long drawers under their slacks, and some who find a suit or pyjamas under their outer gear is the best way of keeping the cold out. There is one winter golfer I know, who turned up on a bleak January morning kitted up in vest and pants, pyjamas, over-trousers, fisherman's heavy knit stockings, flannelette shirt, three pullovers, one gabardine winterproof jacket, scarf, gamekeeper's hat and heavy motoring gloves. Additionally, he carried in his trouser pocket one portable hand-heating instrument. How he was able to swing a club in that sort of garb I will never know, but it did not deter his enthusiasm.

But there are no ends to which the winter golfer will go to better his opponent's battle against the elements. I never dreamt that I would see the day when an opponent in a winter fourball would turn up in a balaclava helmet and kapok mountaineering jacket. If he had blackened his face and substituted a rifle for his golfing bag, he would have passed easily for a war-time commando.

The winter golfer in his cocoon of umpteen woollies undergoes a remarkable transformation when the weather changes and the mists give way to the warmth of spring and summer sunshine. He disrobes almost as dramatically as a strip dancer. Off come helmet, jacket, woollies, scarves, gloves, and the once formidable, heavily-geared figure emerges like a butterfly in the most outrageous display of colours. The contrast is quite startling.

Perhaps Tony Jacklin with his mauve slacks and shirt, or Brian Barnes in his gay pullovers and red-and-white shoes has something to do with it. The club golfer seems to feel that if the stars dress up so can he. He may not play like a Palmer, but he is going to do his level best to look like one.

So we come to the boys in the summer! Fine linen trousers are a must. They are basic to the outfit and the more vivid the colours the better. So we get the palest blues, greens, oranges and purples, all beautifully tailored. And with the slacks come the T-shirts, the V-shirts, the crew neck shirts, the roll neck shirts, all in various designs with a choice of stripes, spots, diamonds, contrasting collars and contrasting arm bands.

Casual spectators might think that this is golf dress gone mad, for on a sunny summer's day there is more colour to be seen on the local golf course than on Brighton beach. But it does not stop with the primary colours. There are shirts in Hawaiian design and hue; shirts that look like pyjama jackets; shirts that look like ladies' blouses; shirts that look like cast-off cushion covers. And all this is crowned by a variety of colourful headgear. In the old days, the well-dressed golfer wore a flat cap on his head. But how we have progressed sar-

Crikey! – What did I do right?

torially since then! Most caps are linen, lightweight and gay, with huge brims to ward off the sun – so a crowd of golfers moving resolutely along the fairways sometimes look for all the world like a gang of jockeys out for an afternoon stroll.

Even the 'Jockey cap' comes in various shapes, high crown, low crown, square crown, with badges, without badges. Then there are the light straw hats long favoured by the veteran American, Sam Snead. Most of them have bands of gay coloured ribbon and large size badges (usually crossed golf clubs). Mind you, a bit of cheating often goes on here for a Majorcan straw hat picked up on holiday for about six bob can look just as impressive on the course as the real Macoy.

Does this revolution in dress help to improve the club golfer's game? Well, I don't know about his game, but I am sure it lifts his morale. He may go out on the course dressed up like Gary Player and return a medal card of 107. His golf may have been excruciating, but he has enjoyed looking the part.

Men's dress in golf has changed over the years, but never quite so dramatically as in the last decade. In the old days it was a jacket and plus-fours; then cardigan and plus-fours. There were periods of plus-twos, Oxford bags, checked trousers and drab grey flannels. But it was the emergence of Carnaby Street that really ushered in the era of the colourful golfer. Its influence on male fashions soon percolated down to the sporting set. It is true that Max Faulkner, former British Open Champion, made a brave effort in years after the war to brighten the golfing scene with his gay outfits, but he was in many ways regarded as an eccentric dresser on the course. Not so today.

As far as the future is concerned, I am sure that some summer soon we are going to see the emergence of Bermuda shorts for the British club golfer. Then we will have a plethora of coloured stockings or socks and all the problems of matching up hat, shirt, shorts, socks and shoes.

Today the ghosts of Vardon, Braid and Taylor in the golfers' Valhalla must ponder, perplexed, as they survey the rainbowed humans that attach themselves to the end of a golf club.

On the other hand, to look good is to feel good and to feel good means that you're half-way there to trying to break bogey. But in this age of topsy-turvy values, one cannot help thinking that this same argument could apply to a band of boys on one municipal course who still find the game just as relishing in vest, braces and gym shoes.

11 Either You Laugh or You Don't

Patrick Smartt

'It is almost superfluous to remark that in all games there must be something serious; otherwise they could all be watched and played with advantage in a Palladium "Crazy Week" or in the circus. A close-fought final in an Amateur Championship is a terrific sight and sensation – a thing of awful hopes and of audible silences; and if, when the champion, hunted to the thirty-sixth green, found a fat man in a dented bowler hat asleep by the flag, few of us in the crowd would find space in our minds to enjoy the joke to the full.'

So wrote the late R. C. Robertson-Glasgow many years ago. That he could conjure up such a situation, superbly improbable, leaves one in no doubt that he would have been one of the few able to 'enjoy the joke to the full'. I have prayed that it might happen ever since I read that piece. That it has not is, perhaps, fortunate, since I should have been reduced to hysteria and frowned upon by those who hold with J. H. Taylor's dictum that golf was not meant to be funny. It depends on how you look at it. J.H. was, of course, playing for his livelihood.

Humour is a ticklish business. I have referred to my dictionary for a definition of it, and found so many uses set down so solemnly that it became funny. The general, everyday assumption is that it is something to cause laughter. But, here's the rub, senses of humour differ. Why, for example, is an air-shot a cause for mirth, and a fluffed approach not? It is not uncommon to hear the remark that someone ' has no sense of humour '. While they may be less prone to laughter, they have their own brand and consider that of others to be facetious or childish.

The ludicrous and pompous are my favourites. An inability to appreciate an amusing situation can be funnier than the incident. Some years ago I was engaged upon research into the early history of Sussex Golf Clubs formed before the turn of the century. My information of the early days came from a book of press cuttings by an unknown journalist writing about 1902. His portentous accounts, without the glimmer of a smile, of two splendid occasions greatly add to them.

' The first competition took place in the Spring of 1890, when the greens were, owing to a long succession of easterly winds, in a fiery condition. Added to this, one green situated on a sloping hillside had been excessively rolled, and the hole being placed at the top edge of the green and there being no level space round the hole, it was impossible to putt the ball up to the hole and lay it dead. The consequence was that when the ball pitched at the foot of the green and the approach shot was attempted to be putted up to the hole it rolled down the hill and was further away after the putt than it was at the commencement.'

So much for the wordy curtain raiser. Now for the episode. 'One of the first to attempt the putt was the late Mr A. J. Lewis, and, after putting courageously 156 times without holing out, he retired from the competition. Many players attempted the putt by running up beyond the hole, but on their attempting to putt downhill the ball gained greater impetus and rolled to the bottom of the hill.' (I wonder what a modern editor's blood pressure would be after reading such a repetition of the obvious: my interpolation.) 'Indeed, there was quite a path by the side of this green worn by the heavy feet of earnest golfers in walking up and down the hill. Eventually the only man who holed out was the captain, who succeeded in winning the hole in 138 strokes, and, being the only competitor who returned a card, won the competition.'

The words ' earnest golfers ' for players whose putts ran into the hundreds on one hole must be the ultimate in labels. Perhaps our unknown scribe was not fully acquainted with the game of golf. He writes of winning the hole in what must have been a medal round. We have not done with him yet. In his account of an incident at another club, reminiscent of the knock-about comedies in the days of silent films, it looks as if a sub-editor stepped in, for the cross-head of the paragraph reads: ' Some Humours of the Scrap Book.' Perhaps I do the writer injustice: it reads:

' For instance, it is recorded that on September 4th

1896, a member, playing the pump hole, was standing on the trough by the pump when he made a stroke which resulted in his turning an involuntary back somersault into the waters of the steep trough.' To my irreverent mind you cannot ask for more than that.

That last is a typical example of British humour. We are not cruel, nor are we malicious, but the misfortunes of others, provided no serious hurt is done, will always raise a laugh. It has something to do with the unexpected and sudden, like a man slipping on a banana skin. Perhaps as a race we never quite grow up.

On one occasion I was playing a friendly match with a member who was left-handed. We were moving calmly along the 11th fairway, enjoying the sunshine and the glory of the gorse in full bloom, when a benevolent looking bullterrier (they always look kindly and not over-intelligent) appeared. It wandered up to me, took a sniff at my trousers and after giving me what can best be described as a courteous nod passed on. Then it approached my companion, whose back was turned, and bit him sharply in the calf, drawing blood from the leg and a rush of it to the face of the victim. Perhaps the animal agreed with Harry Vardon who is alleged to have said he never saw a left-hander worth a damn!

Pain had been inflicted, which should have evoked sympathy. I can only say I was sorely put to it in disguising my amusement. Then the lady owner arrived, and in skittish tones remarked to the afflicted man: '*Isn't he a naughty dog.*' No more need be said, save that my wounded opponent won the next four holes. Engulfing waves of uncontrollable laughter are not an aid to good golf.

Another dog was responsible for a further silent film comedy. A beautifully golf-trained black labrador was with her master in a four-ball game. The setting is a green, and master is preparing to putt. Vicky, for that was her name, suddenly developed the fidgets and walked across behind him. There was a reverberating bellow of ' SIT DOWN '. The scene was enacted several times to the intense amusement of the rest of us. Finally, since her overwrought owner gave every indication of having a convulsion, I seized her collar. All was silence and expectancy. The master's putter had just started on the back-swing when there came the startling sound of a 12-bore, fired by a rabbiter, unseen behind the gorse bushes. No wonder the putt did not drop.

Talking of shooting, a funny thing happened to me in the clubhouse. I was secretary at the time. Myxamatosis was rife in the rabbit world, and I had borrowed a gun so as to put those poor devils I saw out of their misery. One evening in high summer while standing on the house terrace I observed two rabbits on the first teeing-ground. The windows of the men's club-room opened onto the terrace. Inside were four tables of bridge being played by elderly members. The tables were of the old, heavy type.

In order not to disturb them, I took a circuitous route to my office, fetched the gun and returned the same way.

I fired both barrels from just outside the windows. It was a memorable shambles. Cards scattered all over the floor, chairs overturned, and members nursing bruised thighs which had struck the tables as they rose involuntary from their chairs.

When you have a collection of retired members from the armed forces and tea planters from the East, there are some remarkable expletives in languages other than basic English, once described by Winston Churchill as: 'A few remarks of a general character, mostly beginning with the earlier letters of the alphabet.' It cost a lot in consolatory drinks, but one has one's moments.

While on the subject of animals on the course, I have a life-long regret that I was not a spectator at Durban when the players, passing with some umbrage through a herd of cattle, suddenly spotted among them a rhinoceros. In a flash one and all were up trees, golf clubs abandoned in a heap on the ground. The Darwin theory had come into its own again. The animal was dispatched by a policeman with a rifle.

Sooner or later, if you have been connected with a great game for fifty years some funny things are going to happen on the way to the clubhouse. Not necessarily your own club.

There can be few things more discerning than to pull up in a secluded road and find yourself alongside a large cargo ship. We were on our way to Royal Lytham & St Annes for the Open. In the darkness of a near tropical storm in mid-morning – headlights on – we misread a signpost indicating that we turned left. We should have crossed a bridge first. It was, we supposed, the Manchester Ship Canal.

That's the word I was looking for! – provoking

A companion and I were pursing our way through a maze of rural lanes, vainly seeking a club in the depths of Sussex. Heartened by the appearance of a rustic, battered felt hat, fringe beard and all, we asked him the way. He was a Greek, deficient in any knowledge of the English language. Coming upon another wayfarer we agreed upon odds of 6 to 4 on that he would prove to be deaf. He was. Some miles on, the sight of hospital patients taking an airing in bathchairs raised our hopes. It was a lunatic asylum; the pushers and sitters of identical intelligence quota – unless you grant the sitter a point for common sense. All true!

It is trite but true to say golf is full of the unexpected. Tropical sunshine, whispering palm trees and a Scottish friend and I playing. A black figure in prison garb came running on to the course at a speed which would have gained him a gold medal anywhere; a furlong behind, completely outpaced, were two black policemen. The Scot dropped his club, and though well past forty brought his man down with a flying tackle that would have had Murrayfield on its feet. In no time, the caddies *and* the prisoner were rolling on the ground with laughter. The police permitted themselves a broad smile. That is Africa.

My most cherished moment took place during a committee meeting. One of the members was aged and deaf. We were discussing some green committee matter, when the old boy suddenly came to life: ' Let me see, it must have been 1912 or 1913, when Anstruther, or was it General Strumbumbleton ... no, couldn't be him, he'd had a stroke by then. Doesn't matter. Anyway the fellah ran away with the club cook. Shockin' business. We had the hell of a time finding another cook.'

Unbelievable, but true!

(An abbreviated version of the 156 putts appeared in *Golf Monthly*, and the traffic incidents were included in a piece in *Course and Club House*. I am obliged to the Editors for permission to reproduce them.)

12 How Lucky We Are
Geoffrey Cousins

He stalks on to the teeing-ground with a lordly air and a big bag full of shining clubs. He takes from the ball-pocket the missile of his choice and strips off the wrapper, which is thrown negligently into the teebox. The shining white ball is placed on a teepeg driven into the turf, the driver taken from the bag and its head-cover is removed. The solemn preliminaries to the drive are almost complete.

The ball shivers slightly on its plastic perch, and well it might, for the only certainty about its fate is that it will be hard. At best, if the striker is an expert, it will get a hearty smack in the middle of the back and hurtle through the air for 250 yards before landing with a bump and rolling forwards to a gentle rest, which is only the prelude to another smack from some other weapon in the player's armoury. At worst, if at the mercy of a rabbit, it will get a clout on the head and shoot forwards at grass level to finish in the rough with a nasty weal on its hitherto flawless cover. In this case it will suffer much damage and many indignities before, battered beyond repair, it ends its career in the depths of a pond or the gloomy recesses of a wood.

The expert's ball will suffer many blows but mostly clean ones, and relief may come after no more than nine holes, when it is exchanged for another and relegated to the practice bag with a good chance of many long rests. No such happy release is possible for the rabbit's ball, unless it can spin itself out of bounds or get lost in the early stages. Rabbits are not addicted to practice bags and usually regard a ball as serviceable, no matter how many cuts and bruises it bears, until it bursts or disappears.

But the ball, whether used by scratch man or duffer, remains an insignificant nonentity – one of millions of similar spheres which come from the factories to go their several ways. It rests meekly on its teepeg awaiting a blow to be delivered by a human being whose mind is occupied solely by the desire to despatch it as far and as straight as possible. It is too much to expect that the golfer will, in the course of his preparation for the act, ponder on the character of the round white object he is about to assault. If he did he might begin to appreciate how much the chances of beating his handicap depend on the excellence of an intricate mechanism.

Despite its vegetable and mineral background there is something almost human about the modern golf ball. It has a heart which the makers call a core, and round this are its muscles – yards of rubber thread and tape wound under tension. Its skin is a composition cover and the dimples in its face are given cosmetic treatment with fine white paint and bright coloured numerals or symbols. It even has a name, shared, it is true, with millions of others, but a name which gives it standing as a member of a well-known and respected family.

Let the golfer compare this beautiful example of modern technology and chemical expertise with its predecessors, and be thankful that he plays the game in the twentieth century. The 'featherie' and the 'guttie' were no doubt the best products of their respective eras, but quite inadequate when judged by modern standards. The featherie was feather-brained and the guttie had no guts. The Scottish habit of using the affectionate dimunitive to describe both animate and inanimate possessions was never more misapplied than in the case of the feather-stuffed ball and its solid gutta-percha successor.

No one would want to make a featherie nowadays and the task would be virtually impossible, anyway. For one thing, it seems that a top-hat full of feathers and the skin from a cow were pre-requisites. Supposing one found a friend actually owning a top-hat, would he be willing to lend it for so dubious an experiment? And would a neo-Elizabethan topper hold enough feathers for the job, seeing that the early Victorian measure was a 'lum hat', or what our Sassenach forbears would have called a 'stove-pipe'? As for the natural objects involved in the process, it was probably quite easy in those free-ranging days to gather feathers and skin a cow. Just try walking around one of the modern battery chicken farms with a top hat or sidling up to a pedigree Jersey with a penknife, and see what would happen.

But even if all the ingredients are ready to hand, there would be the problem of making a little roundish bag

He's improving! – the divots are getting further and further apart

out of segments of leather, leaving one small gap through which the feathers can be pushed. If, pondering on this ancient variation of the quart-in-a-pint-pot poser, you imagine the worker taking a handful of light downy feathers from the lum hat and putting them one by one into the little bag, while playful eddies of wind cause other feathers to float around the workshop, you have a very poor idea of the ingenuity of those old-time crafts-men. They simply boiled the feathers – not in the top hat, of course – and so reduced them to the proper degree of submission to the stuffing operation. When all the feathers had disappeared – and getting the last of them stowed away must have been a stenuous job for the operator – the gap was closed. Then the whole affair was hammered and pressed into something like a sphere, although more often than not it turned out to be a spheroid with ovoidal tendencies.

Try, modern golfer, to imagine the aero-dynamics of a (fairly) round stitched leather object crammed with feathers in varying degrees of tension, and wonder how far and straight it would have flown under your direction. I have used the epithet feather-brained for obvious reasons. Such a ball would fly somewhat erratically at the muddled dictation of the feathers inside it, and if an ill-aimed blow with a club or collision with the flint chanced to split the skin, its brains would be scattered over the landscape. Then bang would go 'half-a-croon', which was the average price of a well-made featherie 125 years or so ago. Since this was also the price of a bottle of the best Scotch in those good old days, one can imagine the horror with which the average golfer viewed the wreckage of a burst featherie, and the amount of time and energy he would spend searching for one lost among the whins.

It is easy to understand why featheries were bought only by well-to-do golfers. Less affluent addicts combined ingenuity and economy in the search for inexpensive substitutes, unless they were fortunate enough to find a 'lost' ball. Anything approximately round and sound would serve, and size did not matter, because the rules of golf then were concerned with what happened on the course and there was no nonsense about the measurements or design of impedimenta. The Scottish golfer in the featherie age did not care whether his missile was 1.62 inches or 2.62 inches so long as it flew fairly straight and lasted a reasonably long time.

I suppose the industrial revolution anyway would have thrown up some useful and economic substitute for the featherie long before the advent of the rubber-core ball (rubberie?) at the end of the nineteenth century, but it is possible that our grandfathers might have been using the featherie well into the naughty nineties if accident had not placed in an enquiring golfer's hands a piece of solid gutta-percha. It seems that a professor of theology at St Andrews University, named Paterson, received from India a statuette of a Hindu god. It was customary in those days to use gutta-percha for the protection of fragile goods exported from India, and the learned and devout gentleman was intrigued by the hard yet resilient feel of the packing round his statuette. He applied his mind to the idea of using pieces of the melted material as golf balls, and from that empiric start, in 1845, was developed a ball which brought about the first big revolution in the game.

There is no need now to question the ethics of a reverend professor acquiring an Indian idol. If he had any conscience in the matter it must have been salved later by the knowledge that he had conferred a boon on the golfing community. For gutta-percha balls, made at first by heating suitable pieces and rolling them by hand on a board, and later by pressing them in moulds, brought the cost of golf down with a bump, so that the game became within the reach of everyone. The ball-makers, once they had been converted, which meant when they had exhausted their stocks of featheries, found they could produce a dozen gutties in the time occupied in making one featherie and with far less sweat and toil. Moreover the guttie had ten times the durability of the featherie. It did not travel so far, being less resilient, and it was not so easy to play off the turf or from the rough, but it lasted longer and if lost did not leave such a large hole in the pocket. True, it got harder with age and sometimes broke into pieces, but there was a rule to cover this contingency – the spot occupied by the largest piece was the place to drop a substitute ball. Gutties also got hammered out of shape and suffered cuts from iron clubs, but immersion in hot water, repressing in moulds and repainting restored them to mint condition.

So golf went merrily along the guttie for 50 years, until a Mr Coburn Haskell in America developed and introduced a ball with elastic wound round a core and

Er! – I suppose it *is* rather ambiguous

enclosed in a gutta-percha cover. With traditional conservatism British golfers looked at it suspiciously and there was even some talk of making it illegal. But Sandy Herd won the Open Championship in 1902 using the Haskell, and in a very short time the guttie suffered the fate it had inflicted on the featherie half-a-century earlier.

The rubberie is now the plaything of millions all over the world. If only some of them sometimes would spare a thought for those who played with featheries and gutties, enduring the shortcomings of both, and so kept alive the tender plant of world golf in readiness for the blossoming induced by the inventive Mr Haskell. But if we know our fellow-golfers, that's the last thought they'll have in their minds.

13 What is Golf?
Webster Evans

Perhaps it would be easier to ask: 'What isn't golf?' I know it is a four-letter game, but it certainly is not some of the things it has been described as being in the past. Take the following, for instance. In 1869 (the year that the Liverpool, later Royal Liverpool, Club was founded at Hoylake) a book called *Manly Games for Boys* assured its young and ·no doubt innocent readers that 'golf, or bandy ball, is much played in Scotland and the northern parts of England, and is a very excellent game, probably introduced by the Romans'.

Any number of persons, went on the anonymous author, may engage in a game of golf. 'Each player has a straight-handed ash bat, the lower part of which is slightly curved; the object of the game is to drive a small hard ball into certain holes in the ground, and he who soonest accomplishes this wins the game.'

This already conjures up a delightful picture – of a game being played at, say, Sunningdale on a Sunday after-noon – but now the author goes deeper into the niceties (or mysteries) of the game. 'I am not aware of any set of rules having been fixed for the government of golf,' he admits, but explains the general idea thus: 'Two, four or any number of players form themselves into sides, and then fix the golf-lengths, which often extend over three or four miles, especially in winter time, when the game is played on the ice. At various intervals golf-holes are formed, into which the ball must be struck; each party, as in football, endeavouring to drive the ball in an opposite direction.' Are you with me so far?

Finally he tells us that 'you may see golf played on Blackheath occasionally by the young Scots who form the association known as the London Golf Club. Some years since I was present at a golf match on the heath, and a very exciting sight it was, I assure you.' To see Messrs Palmer, Jacklin, Nicklaus and half a dozen others engaging in this game would be a very exciting sight, too.

Uninitiated writers in the old days seem to have been obsessed with the fallacy of speed in golf. A year after the first American golf club – the St Andrews Club of Yonkers-on-Hudson in the state of New York – had been founded in 1888, a long description of the game appeared in the *Philadelphia Times*. It is far from being a 'dude game', the writer said, adding: 'No man should attempt to play golf who has not good legs to run with and good arms to throw with, as well as a modicum of brain power to direct his play.' I like 'a modicum'!

He goes on: 'It is also, by nature of the game itself, a most aristocratic exercise, for no man can play at golf who has not a servant at command to assist him.' Apart from the servant, you also need 'a very large expanse of uncultivated soil'. Having found this (where, he does not

suggest), 'the first thing necessary is to dig a small hole, perhaps one foot or two feet deep and about four inches in diameter. Beginning with this hole, a circle is devised that includes substantially the whole of the links. About once in 500 yards of this circle another hole is dug.' Are you still with me – even if wondering how on earth you get the ball out of the two-foot-deep hole?

Now there are the 'eleven implements of the game' – a ball ('just small enough to fit comfortably into the hole dug in the ground') and ten clubs. Each player places his ball at the edge of the starting hole and 'when the word has been given to start, he bats his ball as accurately as possible towards the next hole. As soon as it is started in the air, he runs forward in the direction which the ball has taken, and his servant, who is called a "caddie", runs after him with all the other nine tools in his arms.' Got it?

The basic object of the game, we are told, 'is to put the ball in the next hole, spoon it out and drive it forward to the next further one before his opponent can accomplish the same end'. The servant or caddie follows his master as closely as possible – 'generally at a dead run'. Thus it will be seen that the caddie 'really gets as much exercise out of the sport as his master'.

Spectators are sometimes present, we learn, but normally (and wisely) stand well away, for the ball may fall among them 'and cause some temporary discomfort' – presumably like a black eye. It is not perhaps surprising to find the writer stressing that golf is 'not a game which would induce men of elegance to compete in, but

those who have strong wind and good muscle may find
it a splendid exercise for their abilities'.

Oddly enough, the writer of this article agrees with the
author of *Manly Games for Boys* about the lack of rules
in the manly game for men: 'There are no codified rules
according to which the game is played.' The complete
Rules of Golf were, however, set out in the first American
book devoted to the game – *Golf in America*, published
in 1895. Some misapprehension about speed still lingered,
for the author, James P. Lee, after saying that 'a new
game has lately been added to the list of our outdoor
sports', assures his readers that 'there is no racing or any
effort to accomplish a hole in less time than your opponent'.

Even in England in the early years of this century
there were doubts about the objective of the exercise. A
stop-press report in a London evening paper after Jack
White had scored a record 75 in the 1904 Open Championship gave readers this startling news: 'White
breaks record at Sandwich, going round in 7 minutes
5 seconds.'

In the late 1890s there were signs of interest in high
circles, even if there were still misapprehensions. In *Golf
Illustrated*, dated 17th March 1899, it was revealed that
'the latest recruit to the ranks of golf is H.R.H. the
Prince of Wales, who has been playing at Cannes under
the tuition of the Grand Duke Michael of Russia'. The
fact that the Grand Duke's notorious lack of skill made
it a case of the blind leading the blind didn't prevent the
paper saying in the issue of 31st March that 'the Prince

is described as being a very promising player with a free and steady swing'.

I imagine he would have lost his steady swing – and his dignity – if he ever indulged in his wife's version of the game. The Princess of Wales (the future Queen Alexandra) had a few holes laid out in Sandringham Park. According to Georgina Battiscombe's *Queen Alexandra* (1969), she 'never grasped the rules of the game, regarding it as a kind of hockey allowing of much light-hearted scrummaging, the winner being the player who first succeeded in propelling his or her ball into the hole, regardless of the number of strokes played'.

This royal version was anything but a 'dude game' and would hardly have appealed to Oscar Wilde, who once remarked that football 'is all very well as a game for rough girls, but is scarcely suitable for delicate boys'. All the same, he once persuaded his wife that he had taken up golf. In a letter to an American friend she reported that Oscar 'has become mad about golf, and spends two or three hours on the links every day, and this is so good for him'. Hesketh Pearson, who quotes this story in his *Life of Oscar Wilde* (1946), says that Oscar's 'description of the game would have amazed a golfer; but one wonders whether he did the thing properly and carried a bag of clubs to the Café Royal every morning'.

It would be nice, all the same, to think of Oscar, dressed in knickerbockers and velvet coat, playing golf for its therapeutic qualities. And there is no doubt that golf can do the player a power of good. David Robertson

It ensures that every drive travels at least 4 feet

Forgan, a member of the famous old Scottish ball and club making firm, put it nicely when he wrote: 'Golf is a test of temper, a trial of honour, a revealer of character. It affords a chance to play the man and act the gentleman. It means going into God's out-of-doors, getting close to nature, fresh air, exercise, a sweeping away of mental cobwebs, genuine re-creation of the tired tissues. It is a cure for care – an antidote to worry. It includes companionship with friends, social intercourse, opportunities for courtesy, kindliness and generosity to an opponent. It promotes not only physical health but moral force.'

The other side of the coin was shown by a certain Dr A. S. Lamb, of Canada's McGill University, who claimed (I only hope with tongue in cheek) that golf 'increases the blood pressure, ruins the disposition, spoils the digestion, induces neurasthenia, hurts the eyes, callouses the hands, ties kinks in the nervous system, debauches the morals, drives men to drink or homicide, breaks up the family, turns the ductless glands into internal warts, corrodes the pneumogastric nerve, breaks off the edges of the vertebrae, induces spinal meningitis and progressive mendacity, and starts angina pectoris'.

We seem to have got some way away from the theme of What is Golf? Never mind; we shall probably never know, however much is written or spoken about the game. My copy of Dr Samuel Johnson's Dictionary merely says that golf is 'a game played with a ball and a club or bat'. True enough, but what a lot remains unsaid in this brief sentence.

I began quoting from *Manly Games for Boys* and I cannot do better than end by giving the anonymous author another chance to air his knowledge. Under the heading of ' Hockey ', he tells us that ' this is also a capital game for wintry weather and may be played by any number of boys. The only implements required are a few stout sticks and a good bung or ball. In Scotland it is immensely popular under the name of golf, from which it differs only in detail.'

I can only think I haven't really been playing golf all these years! Indeed, perhaps it would be less of a dude game played without rules, with any number of players driving the ball (or bung) in opposite directions over fixed golf-lengths on the uncultivated soil, the whole thing carried out at a dead run ...